FORK SOCIAL MEDIA AND THE ALGORITHM IT RODE IN ON (JAILBIRD STORIES)

FORK SOCIAL MEDIA AND THE ALGORITHM IT RODE IN ON (JAILBIRD STORIES)

SUDI (RICK) KARATAS

Disclaimer

These stories were sent or told to the author, none of their facts were changed, some were edited for length and grammar.

Sudirick Books/ Sudi "Rick"Karatas
www.sudirick.com
Sudirick@aol.com

Copy editing by Jo Bird

Cover design by Tim Heagerty of Heagerty Designs
back cover author photo by Larry Weissman

Library of Congress control number   TXu 2-417-929

Dedication

This book is dedicated to all those in my Facebook family who have spent time in "prison cyber cells".

Also, to my real-life family including: my nieces and nephews, Jamie, Jo Jo, and Tony Gullo, Brian, Kara and Danny Dougherty,

my siblings Sibel, Suzie, Kenan and their spouses, Chris, Doc and Michele and my brother Kevin.

My mom Terry, my late father Nevzat, my partner Carlos and my relatives in the U.S.A. and in Turkey,

for their love and support

CONTENTS

VIII - CONTENTS

INTRODUCTION

You make an innocent, humorous comment or post on Facebook, and faster than you can say, "Zuckerberg is a turd," you're restricted, banned, punished, and exiled to Facebook Jail. You can't post or comment. Sometimes, the sentence is a few days, sometimes, thirty days, and sometimes, sixty days or more. No court trial, no district attorney, no 'innocent until proven guilty.' Your judge is an algorithm that doesn't understand sarcasm, humor, or satire and lacks common sense. You have no way to get the fake charges dropped. You usually don't even get a warning, just Bam! You're thrown into the virtual slammer. No opportunity to appeal or fight it, even though they pretend there is.

I am an 'ex-con' of Facebook jail. Me, who never even had detention or was sent to the principal's office in High School, has been a prisoner of Facebook a few times. Well, I'd had enough of being wrongfully accused, locked up and denied my freedom! I realized there were thousands, if not millions—okay, maybe not millions—of others who have suffered the same experience where much frustration and harm was caused by needless banning and Facebook restrictions.

I collected some of the most ridiculous reasons Facebook users were locked up. I gave out or emailed people a questionnaire to fill out asking, "How many times have you been in Facebook jail and for what reason? How did being banned or restricted affect or hurt you? Did you try to file an appeal? How did that go?" Facebook is now called Meta but the app is still Facebook, and many users still call it that.

I chose the most bizarre and absurd stories from those Facebook users who were sent up the 'Facebook River' by the 'Facebook Fuzz' or the Poo Poo Po Po, as I call them. I hope the stories will make you laugh and entertain you. More importantly, I hope the absurdity will point out how ridiculous Facebook is sometimes and the harm it has caused. They need to take heed and change their ways. In the words of Sandy in the musical Grease, played by the late Olivia Newton-John, one of my all-time favorite entertainers, "You better shape up," Facebook (Meta)!

I hope you enjoy reading these stories from all the Ex-cons and perps.

Sudi (Rick) Karatas

CHAPTER 1

A Monopoly's Community Standards for Dummies

WHAT IS FACEBOOK JAIL?

Facebook jail is a popular slang term that describes a temporary ban from posting on Facebook. These bans are slapped on users who intentionally or accidentally violate Facebook's Community Standards. The length of a Facebook jail sentence can vary from twenty-four hours to multiple days or even weeks. During their sentence, users cannot post on their Timeline, in groups, or comment on other posts. They may also be barred from sending messages or friend requests. The reasons users get banned include posting too much in a short time, using certain words in posts, or even being reported by another user.

There are now several Facebook Jail groups users have formed on Facebook with thousands of members including Official Facebook Jail, which has more than 7,000 members.

MONOPOLY

No, I'm not talking about the board game where you can buy Boardwalk, Park Place, tiny green houses and red hotels. This monopoly is Facebook, and we are all prisoners of their algorithms that have the IQ of a Farmville potato—Is that stupid game even on Facebook anymore? If Facebook were the board game, you would probably need a hundred get out of jail free cards. On Facebook, you're sent directly to jail. You don't pass go or collect $200. There are no handcuffs, but your online voice is muzzled, and you have no 'chance' to defend yourself – pun intended.

FACEBOOK COMMUNITY STANDARDS

Facebook Community Standards are divided into six sections:

1. Violence and criminal behavior
2. Safety
3. Objectionable content
4. Integrity and authenticity;
5. Respecting intellectual property
6. Content-related requests.

FACEBOOK COMMUNITY STANDARDS EXPLAINED:

Here are some of the most common reasons people end up in Facebook jail:

1. **Posting too quickly:** You can get flagged when posting the same information too quickly.
2. **Sending too many friend requests in one day:** Especially if you don't know the people. The platform will likely block your account. The same goes for joining Facebook groups too fast.
3. **Posting inappropriate content:** Posting sexually suggestive content or nudity on Facebook is prohibited. Avoid posting self-harm content, hate speech, or credible threats to groups or individuals, including racist or other discriminatory content.
4. **Too much tagging:** when you create too many links to other profiles.

5. **Using spam images or videos:** If Facebook or Google has marked images or videos as spam, and you use them in your posts and are thought to be spamming others, this can land you in Facebook jail.

6. **Logging in with different accounts:** If you log into Facebook at the same time using different accounts, even a business page, this can trigger a block on your account. You should only use one account on one device and a different one if you need to have two accounts open simultaneously.

7. **Being spammy:** Adding people you don't know or using a business name for your personal account. Don't add spammy links, don't send bulk messages, don't excessively post images and links to people's timelines, and don't continually post identical content to different groups or places.

8. **Using automated software:** If you like or comment on posts at a very fast pace, Facebook will likely block your account.

9. **Using fake or imposter accounts:** If someone reports that your account is fake or impersonating someone else's account, Facebook won't hesitate to block it permanently.

10. **Fraud with payments through Facebook:** Suspicious payments are among recently emerging reasons for bans on Facebook. If you make a payment through a fraudulent card, the payment will be reversed, and your account will be instantly banned.

11. **Hacking other accounts:** Unauthorized access to someone's profile, often with malicious intent.

12. **Posting copyrighted material:** If you post copyrighted content without the owner's consent, you will encounter a ban on Facebook. Copyrighted material includes music, videos, or images you don't have permission to use.

Author's thoughts: In Facebook's defense (I know what you are thinking, why should they get a defense when we don't) rules are made to protect people, but sometimes rules end up punishing the wrong people, or because of the actions of a few, many have to suffer. In my opinion, Facebook is too cheap—like most corporations—to hire enough people to go through the cases. They make billions of dollars and don't spend any hiring humans who could clear up many of these issues for their users.

Sentencing

This varies depending on the "crime" and how many times you've been banned before. For most violations on Facebook, strikes will lead to the following restrictions:

One strike: You'll get a warning since this is your first strike.
Two to six strikes: You'll be restricted from specific features, like posting in groups, for a limited time.
Seven strikes: You'll get a one-day restriction from creating content, which includes posting, commenting, creating a page, and more.
Eight strikes: You'll get a three-day restriction from creating content.
Nine strikes: You'll get a seven-day restriction from creating content.
Ten or more strikes: You'll get a thirty-day restriction from creating content.

Facebook Jail Song

I'm a songwriter, so of course, I had to write a song about my Facebook experience. The lyrics are below.

FACEBOOK JAIL
by Sudi (Rick) Karatas

Verse One:
I saw a post and left a comment
I wrote "Stick a fork in him he's done"
The Meta police didn't get the reference
They thought a violent crime had begun

Before I could even count to three
No rights read to me
A justice system where I can't win
I'm a virtual prisoner once again

Chorus:
If you've been in
Facebook Jail
Raise your hand
Facebook Jail
You're restricted and banned
An innocent post, the algorithm
did not understand
No jury, no judge, no bail
When you're in
Facebook Jail

Verse Two:

I tried so hard to fight the system
Appealed many times but in vain
Sarcasm, humor and satire are not allowed
It's out of control, they've gone insane
It takes everything literally
No ability
To decipher what's real and what's not
Our livelihood in the hands of a bot

Repeat Chorus

Bridge

Let me out, let me out, let me out
I did nothing wrong

All those who've had enough
Help me sing this song
Repeat Chorus
Tag: As the sentences accrue, there's nothing you can do.

Copyright 2022

Johnny Cash wrote the song "Folsom Prison Blues." Another famous crime song was "I Fought the Law, And the Law Won." I guess I fought Facebook, and Facebook won. Or did they? I wrote this book so I might get the last word and last laugh. Hopefully, you, the reader, get some laughs too.

CHAPTER 2

Violence: Facebook Can Shove the Algorithm up its Butt!

We'll start with my story first because, well, I'm the author, and that's how the idea for the book was born. And, like Facebook, I don't have to give you a reason for any of my decisions.

Sudi (Rick) Karatas: What the Fork?

The first time I got banned or put in Facebook jail was when a friend complained about a guy on their page and how he was such a jerk. I commented on his post, "Men are scum." I'm a man, so I was clearly joking, but the algorithm picked up the word "scum," and since it doesn't understand sarcasm or humor, it viewed it as hate speech.

I was arrested and prosecuted and could not comment or post for many days. My friend whose page it was on didn't have an issue with my comment. No one on his page complained, not even anyone named Karen. A human being would have seen it as a harmless comment, but a computer was the police officer here. Later, when I was telling someone on Facebook that I was restricted because I used the word scum, I intentionally spelled it wrong. I wrote 'scuuum' so Facebook wouldn't flag it again, but guess what? I was thrown back in jail with a longer sentence and not allowed to post or comment. I filed an appeal, but of course, nothing came of it.

A few weeks later, someone posted a picture of Donald Trump on TV, and when they held a fork up to his face, it looked like he was behind bars. The person wrote, "I love to see the way he looks behind bars." I commented, "Stick a fork in him, he's done," and I was jailed for promoting violence. Facebook takes everything so literally because it's not a human.

Everyone knows "Stick a fork in it, it's done" is a cooking reference to when the food is fully cooked. In this case I meant his career in politics was done. The algorithm literally thought I meant sticking a fork in someone, causing harm. Some humans are as dumb as Facebook algorithms, I have to say. Well, I don't have to say it, but I choose to. My mouth! My choice!

The word "fork" bothers Facebook and Instagram (also owned by Meta). I once said on Instagram, "Sarah Huckabee speaks with forked tongue, and she can go fork herself," and I got banned temporarily for promoting violence and suicide.

That run-in I had with the Facebook police was the straw that broke this Turkish camel's back and gave me the idea for this book. While writing, I joked on Facebook to someone saying, "Go jump in the Hudson River." Once again, I was restricted from posting on any-one's Facebook pages for thirty days for promoting suicide, which was the furthest thing from my mind. I think my joke was more about the Hudson River being dirty, but the algorithm, like my family, doesn't get my jokes. So, I was up the river for joking about a river.

This wasn't just an inconvenience. It stopped me from posting the date of our next NSAI (Nashville Songwriting Association Inc.) song-writing workshop. I am a coordinator for them and have a Facebook page for our Los Angeles Chapter. I had to contact someone on the page to post for me.

I also couldn't promote my other books, songs, or anything.

Tom Ryan and the "bomb."

Tom is from Philadelphia, PA, and is a theater actor and director. He works in media and arts PR. He's been on Facebook for fourteen years and has been in trouble a few times, but since the new Meta merge, it has been much worse. He has been flagged for reposting from his own memory wall from seven or eight years ago for violating Community Standards. But the time that he says was the dumbest was when he had a stray cat he took care of, and he even brought him into the house at night. The cat slept in the basement, where the exercise equipment was. Tom discovered he had a major flea infestation down there. He tried everything and was talking about it with his friends on Facebook. One friend mentioned that he should get flea bombs and use them. Tom conceded that was his next step. The friend said, "Don't forget you will have to vacuum everything," to which Tom replied, "First, we have to bomb the basement." Within a minute of posting that reply, a box appeared on his post saying he was in violation of Community Standards, inciting violence.

His account was locked for two days. He could not post in any of his groups for an additional forty-eight hours, and his posts went to the bottom of the feed for thirty days. His interaction with friends was limited. He said thank God he didn't have a project that needed daily care. He tried to appeal, but the only thing he got was a pop-up box that asked if he agreed or disagreed with their decision. He said he disagreed. But as usual, with Facebook, he got zero feedback. They don't look at conversations, and there's no one to appeal to. You just have to sit back and take it!

Karen Mamont: Facebook Needs to be Schooled on History

I met Karen—a.k.a. Reverend Martini—at L.A. Fitness in California. She's a realtor, music producer, and promoter for VLV All Night Rock'n Showcase. She was wearing a shirt that said "F*# k Trump." I commented on how much I liked the shirt, and we became instant friends. I sent her a questionnaire to fill out. She had been in Facebook jail numerous times and said she almost wears it like a badge of honor now! One time she was thrown in the "hoosegow" was when a friend posted a picture of a book, *Marriage Advice, by King Henry the 8th*. She laughed because it was ironic that the King, who had six wives, most of whom met a horrible demise by his decree, should give marriage advice! Karen commented to her friend on Facebook, "I don't think Anne Boleyn would agree."

The young woman whose post it was asked, "Who's Anne Boleyn?" Karen answered, "Anne Boleyn was one of King Henry's six wives. He created The Church of England because the Catholic Church would not give him a divorce from his devout Spanish Queen, Catherine of Aragan, to marry his mistress, Anne Boleyn. When Anne failed to give him a male heir, he accused her of adultery and had her head chopped off." That was a historical fact, but the robot thought Karen was promoting violence. She tried to appeal, but there was no human making the decision or coming to the phone for customer service.

Anonymous: Thrown in Jail for Sticking Up for the Police

Sometime in the summer of 2022, a Facebook friend posted a link to an article about how two cops somewhere in Pennsylvania entered a coffee shop and did nothing other than have a uniform on. Some jerk entered and shot them both dead. The Facebook user's comment was something to the effect of, "The perpetrators ought to be publicly hanged as a deterrent." That was it. For that, he was put in Facebook jail for about a month. He could see posts but was unable to post or comment on anyone else's posts. After one month, his jail sentence was lifted.

He thinks what Facebook did to him was ludicrous. He is on there every day, so it was an inconvenience from a social networking standpoint. That said, he could see where they were coming from.

While he's not up on all the details, he read last year that legislation was passed that requires any social networking site to be very strict regarding any post that even alludes to violence. In the big picture, that may be a good thing, considering what a violent, dysfunctional society we have become. And as huge as Facebook is, how could they possibly differentiate between a relatively harmless post like his and someone who is plotting violence?

Author's Thoughts: Don't use the words hang or hung, especially hung, because that can be taken as pornography and violence.

Will Person: A "Time Out" For a Joke About Spanking

Will is from California, a retired Winter Olympic athlete who was a member of the US Olympic bobsleigh team between 1999 and 2007. Will has no idea how many times he's been in Facebook jail and guesses it's more than four but less than ten. One of his best friends, actor Lejon Stewart, made fun of a picture he posted. Will responded, "Lejon, I will marry your mom and become your stepdaddy so I can legally spank you." Boom! He was in handcuffs.

Another time, Will found a post on Facebook, a picture of a young lady lying beside a big screen TV, and the caption said, "Look how much larger my TV is than my dishwasher." Will reposted the picture and received thirty days in Facebook jail. He found the post on Facebook, so why did he get in trouble? He has reported several posts that use the "n" word, and Facebook quickly responds that this does not go against their standards. Will said the ban was eye-opening and a blessing. Every time he logged in and was unable to interact, it was a reminder that he spends too much time on Facebook.

Patrik Simpson: Dressed to Kill

Patrik is the Producer of the show *Gown and Out in Beverly Hills* along with his husband, Pol Atteu, who is a celebrity fashion designer —"Haute Couture" in Beverly Hills. The two also do a podcast called *Undressed with Pol and Patrik.* Patrik has been in the Facebook pokey twice.

The first time was when Pol made a wedding gown for Sheena Shay from the Emmy-nominated reality show *Vanderpump Rules.* When she was in the boutique for one of her fittings, she posted a picture of her wearing the dress. Pol stood in front of her, and Patrik was on the other side. They were blocking her so no one could see the dress. The pic went into *Us Weekly,* and Patrik reposted the article saying, "We're excited Pol is making Sheena's—from the show "Vanderpump Rules" —dress. I can't show you the dress. If I did, I'd have to kill you."

Boom! It was a joke, but they blocked the post, and he was put in Instagram Jail—Instagram is also owned by the same company that owns Facebook—and banned for three days.

CHAPTER 3

Pork and Violence
Don't Mix

Facebook seems to have a big problem with the word pig. I would be afraid to post a picture or video of a Hawaiian Luau on Facebook. They would probably send their SWAT team to take me into custody faster than Porky Pig can say, "Ubitty ubitty, that's all folks!" No idea if I spelled that word right. Apparently, if you compare men to pigs, it's an insult. Pigs probably think it's cool. It's all about perspective, but by now, you know the algorithm doesn't have perspective or common sense. The woman in that TV commercial years ago who sang about bringing home the bacon and frying it up in a pan would probably get banned on Facebook today for promoting violence against pigs.

Michael Vega: Pull the Pork

Michael is an actor & bartender in California. This is his nightmare story. Michael occasionally co-hosted a podcast called *On the Rocks Radio Show with Alexander Rodriguez*. On a particular episode, because of Covid-19 protocols in the studio, he sat in on a zany and fascinating interview with the late Anne Heche and her publicist. Later that evening, he got into a random dialogue on Facebook with a straight cousin from Jersey about having spoken to Anne Heche and what a zany force of nature she was. In typical straight guy fashion, Little Luis, well, that's what they called him as kids, started saying how he'd tap her as he was into older women. Michael answered Luis' horndog response by saying, "Gay or straight men are pigs." Bang! He was slapped with a hate speech restriction for three days! He had already suffered through the twenty-four-hour restriction for a Trump post where he simply said, "Zeig Heil." Michael was like, "What? Is that bad?"

So, an anxious three days passed, and he got back online. He was in a dialogue with someone, and his cousin popped on to say, "Hey, Cuz! Welcome back! Lol." Michael laughed and replied, "Lol men are still pigs!" Bang! He was instantly hit with a week-long restriction. He said he probably asked for it, but he couldn't fathom why a non-specific joke between family members was labeled hate speech. Needless to say, it was a long week. He returned only to get thirty days for joking with a friend about his birthday. Michael joked, "I'm going to slice you through the middle and count the rings." Michael thought that was funny. But nope, he was violently threatening the birthday boy. Bwahaha! Michael said it was the longest month of his life.

Being banned and restricted affected Michael and hurt him. It was during the Covid-19 lockdown, and he lived alone. For many months, Facebook was his only real interaction with friends, family, and colleagues. He was plagued by severe anxiety at the time, as many were. His anxiety became heightened when he couldn't just log on and interact. Breathless and restless, "Thank God for marijuana delivery," he said. He tried to school the bots on the nuances of humor, but to no avail.

Author's thoughts: Again, the problem is how the algorithm takes everything literally. It didn't know that when you cut a tree, you can count the rings to see how old it is. So, the algorithm did not get the joke about slicing him through the middle. It has no sense of humor. Nothing vicious was said, no one was being threatened. Facebook should look for dangerous posts, but the way they do it now is not working. We know there are plenty of posts on Facebook spreading misinformation or offensive and objectionable things, but Facebook doesn't seem to be finding those. They are punishing innocent people. Facebook did not say that "Men are pigs" was false information, just that it was hate speech, so Facebook may actually agree with the statement. I finally started putting asterisks within the words like scum, like this s*um, and pigs like this, p&

Pete Lawson: Pistols and Pork

Pete was the husband of Diane, a college friend of mine. I enjoyed his inspiring book *Keeping The Faith* (*Life Hacks From The Irish Cockroach*), which came out in 2023. He sadly passed away in February 2024.

He had a post on his cancer survivor webpage, www.irishcockroach.com, a site for cancer survivors with a twist of humor and inspirational comments. His post was titled "Running with Pigs." The post was a reflection on facing your fears head-on and not running away from them. Facebook put him in jail when a friend commented on the post, saying, "Shoot first, ask questions later." Pete had no idea of the infraction until they told him his account was locked for a month. That meant he couldn't advertise (Facebook loses revenue?), and it would be pushed down in priority. He was a little concerned about it since cancer survivors read the blog each week, but despite all the warnings, nothing really changed on his blog. Pete thinks Facebook uses quite a bit of AI to review comments, but it's ineffective since the blog was about shooting at wild pigs.

Author's Thoughts: I'm surprised the word cock in cockroach.com didn't get flagged and get Pete banned. These misunderstandings on Facebook about violence, like in Pete's story, made me think about the sketch that aired years ago on Saturday Night Live with Gilda Radner as Roseanne Rosanna Dana. She was complaining that people wanted to get rid of violins, and she didn't understand why. What was so wrong with violins? They make beautiful music. After going on and on complaining about people who wanted to stop violins, it was finally explained to her, "No, not violins. Violence." And she was like, "Oh, never mind". Thanks, Gilda, for the laughs. The algorithm is just as clueless as Rosanne Rosanna Dana.

Also, Pete was joking about shooting first and asking questions later, got in trouble, and was put in Facebook jail. In real life, as I was writing this book in 2023, several people had been shot in this country for accidentally knocking on the door of the wrong house or turning into the wrong driveway. The shooters got off scot-free because of the stand your ground laws. These people shot first before asking questions and weren't punished as much as someone who makes a joke on Facebook about shooting first. I'll bet if you so much as say "Let's shoot the breeze," the algorithm will be on you like brown on rice. Yes, I know the expression is "white on rice," but I don't want to be accused of racism.

Kenny P: Three Little Pigs

Kenny P, an actor, comic and writer from New York City, has been in Facebook jail many times. He guesses fifteen times. Everything from inappropriate jokes or memes in private groups to political arguments in which he used words or phrases that Facebook deemed offensive or hateful. One of the most ridiculous things he's been in jail for was when he posted his opening statement from an old dating profile. It was a humorous description of who he was and what he was looking for, and Facebook told him it was possibly trafficking. After a couple of days, when Facebook realized it wasn't trafficking, they gave it the *green light*—see what I did there—and put it back. One of his incarcerations in Facebook jail was six days for quoting the Three Little Pigs. "Then I'll huff, and I'll puff, and I'll blow your house in.' Once again, the clueless algorithm thought someone was promoting violence who wasn't. Kenny is very social and active on Facebook, not to mention posting where he's performing and other career stuff. So "Yes, it kind of sucked," he said, not being able to promote his gigs. A couple of times, he filed an appeal with their oversight board, which nobody ever oversaw.

Author's Thoughts: I added the phrase "they gave it the green light" after the word trafficking. If you don't think it's funny, bite me. The freedom to say bite me in my book, as opposed to being unable to say that on Facebook, feels wonderful. Of course, I'm not really asking you to bite me. It's an expression that would go over the algorithm's stupid little head. Mike Tyson actually bit someone's ear off, but I bet he's allowed on Facebook.

So, in conclusion, try to avoid using the word pig on Facebook. Not sure if hog is okay.

CHAPTER 4

Wooly Bullying

Bullying is a very serious problem, especially when it happens to kids, and it can sometimes lead to suicide. So again, Facebook is trying to do the right thing and not allow it. But Facebook is like the teacher playing favorites with certain students. Some get off scot-free, and others seem to be targeted. Sometimes, the re-poster is charged with bullying and put in Facebook jail and the person who posted the original content roams around free as a bird. Here are some stories from those accused of bullying who believe they were falsely charged.

Jon Tessler (Lil' Jon) In Big Trouble

Jon lives in Virginia and is a retired Veteran, and all his crimes have been violations of Facebook's Terms of Service. Many of the stories are because the Facebook algorithm does not understand sarcasm or the context of the comments. Jon noticed that certain words could be said, ones that fall under their guidelines for bullying or hateful speech, and nothing would be done about it even when it was reported. But if you comment back in kind—you insult me, I will insult you—the second person always gets flagged and tossed in jail. In 2021, Jon was in Facebook Jail at the beginning of January and was put back in jail for seven consecutive months, sometimes only being out for a few hours. In 2022, he was in jail in January, February, and August.

He said the worst part was there was no way to appeal. Facebook claims their oversight committee will look at cases, but Jon has never seen any of his cases accepted, so there is really no way to fight a ban. He even went as far as to email the head of Facebook's legal department over a group—AxaMonitor—he claims had harassed him and others for more than eight years, and he never even got a response to a detailed email with attached screen shot of the harassment. Jon has also gotten the "We made a mistake, but you still can't post for thirty days" response. Why allow someone to review their comment or post if it doesn't change the outcome? He said that restrictions and bans no longer affect him in any way. He expects to be put in jail these days. He usually uses the time to cut down on groups and cull his friends list.

Joseph R. Nunweiler-Meleka: If the Name Fits, Wear it

In May of 2018 B.C. (Before Covid) Joseph noticed a Facebook user agreeing with everything that the occupant (at the time) of the White House was saying and doing. Joe commented, "Drumpf is a racist, he is misogynistic, xenophobic, cruel to the disabled and the LGBTQ+ community, and if you agree with him, you must also agree with all of his evil policies, you are just as bad as he is." He was reported and placed in Facebook jail for one day for bullying. He said being put in Facebook jail upset him. He was pissed because what he wrote was true. "If you agree with the man and all his policies, you are just as bad as he is." Joe filed an appeal, but they found against him because he had called the President of the U.S. by a name other than his real one. He was disrespectful, so they believed the person who had complained that Joe was a bully.

Author's Thoughts: That President that Joseph called a different name had no problem calling quite a few other people really bad names. Just sayin'!

Anonymous: Suspended For Sarcasm

He/she/they had a friendly discussion with another Facebook user regarding roundabouts (traffic circles where one does not have to make a left-hand turn). They argued in favor of them, suggesting they were an alternative to issuing hunting licenses to hunt idiots making left-hand turns onto a busy street and backing up traffic for half a mile. They suggested hunting licenses as an alternative if municipalities found roundabouts too expensive to construct. They further suggested this step would quite possibly spare us from their children, they would otherwise inflict on society with God knows what other vile and disgusting habits detrimental to the social order and public morals. Their comments were intended facetiously and written in a slightly unhinged tone, in homage to Jonathan Swift's *A Modest Proposal*. They were informed that their account had been suspended because of bullying, hostility, and possible hurtful feelings. The user disagreed with Facebook's decision, although they provided no opportunity for self-defense. A few hours later, they got a message that Facebook had reconsidered and restored their privileges, along with an apology.

Author's Thoughts: This is one of the rare times someone who complained was heard and released from those Facebook prison chains. I wish I knew how they accomplished it, but at least there is a glimmer of hope that it's possible. If sarcasm were really a crime, I'd spend my life in prison.

Jim Seeley: Saying "White Trash" Will Get You Thrown Out!

Jim's first offense, or Crime 1, got him thrown in Facebook jail for three days when he used the term "white trash" in a post. It was flagged as hate speech. Jim said Facebook obviously doesn't understand the concept of context. He is a lower-middle-class Caucasian, so he was not hating on anyone else. He's in that demographic. He uses an amusing example of this from the movie *Rush Hour* to prove his point. Jackie Chan is just learning English and is in the L.A. area. He goes to an African American pool hall. He hears one black guy say to the bartender—also black "What's up, my N word?" They high-five or whatever. Then Jackie goes up to the bartender and tries out the new phrase he's learned with a big smile, thinking he's going to impress the bartender with his knowledge of African American slang. Instead, a big fight breaks out!

Dan Cooke: Burned by Facebook and Almost by a wildfire

Dan, from California, had a guy harassing him and posted on his page about it. He didn't realize it was public. The guy flooded his post with insults and racism, and Dan was banned. Another time, he was banned for calling out other people's racism—white supremacy. He had a lot of trouble reaching out to friends for help when a large wildfire was a few miles from his place and was moving fast. He wanted to take some things to safety, like pets. Everything was fine in the end. He tried to file an appeal, but they kept asking for links to the harassing comments, but he couldn't because Facebook deleted the post with the comments. They destroyed most of the evidence.

CHAPTER 5

Warning: Warning, Danger Will Robinson!

The title of this chapter is a reference to the show from the 1960s, "*Lost in Space,*" where the robot warned young Will Robinson when there was danger. Ironically, today, sixty-plus years later, a robot, or bot as we now call it, is to blame for all these misunderstandings about certain posts. Some people are lucky enough just to get a warning or get flagged. I'm not sure how. It's not like they can bat their eyes or flirt with the Facebook police or show a badge that shows their second cousin's nephew is in the police force, and they let them go. I think Facebook should give more warnings instead of restricting people. Give the users a chance to correct or change the language for any offensive— or what they deem to be offensive—post. And if it is an innocent post that has been mislabeled, there should be someone at Facebook to clear that up.

The following stories are from some lucky bastards who got off with a warning, just a cyber slap on the wrist.

Bruce Laffey

Bruce lives in Los Angeles, and this is his story. He was commenting on a post from someone who had relatives visiting Santa Monica. She told him a few days earlier that she wanted to take them to the Santa Monica restaurant, El Cholo, so he innocently asked them if they went there by just writing two words "El Cholo?". He got flagged! He was never sent to jail, but it was hard to fight back. Baffled, he googled Cholo. This is the Wikipedia definition: Cholo is a loosely defined Spanish term that has various meanings. Its origin is a somewhat derogatory term for people of mixed-blood heritage.

Author's Thoughts: Hay Dios Mio! (Oh My God).

Joe Brown

Joe, a friend who does Real Estate in New York, was exchanging messages with his friend Mark and hadn't seen him for a while. Since they hadn't gotten together recently, he said, "We have to hang Mark." You leave out one little comma and see what happens! Facebook removed the comment, and he got a warning because, of course, the algorithm thought Mark was in danger. It thought Mark was going to be hung. So, Joe posted the message again, saying, "We have to hang out soon."

Kimberlye Gold

Kimberlye is a singer-songwriter. Facebook took down a memory she commented on about an adorable gal named Rose she used to play music for at a memory care retirement gig back in 2014. The post was, "This is my beloved Rose from the Memory Care section of one of my monthly haunts. When I begin each song, she lights up like a candle, and her eyes get wide with excitement and she acts out every word. She turns to whoever is next to her to emphasize whatever she is singing and tries to engage them. And after each song, she looks at me and says, 'Thank you!' So cute. I swear, I am going to kidnap her next time!" Facebook said the post went against their Community Standards and that Kimberlye was threatening danger and violence. She said, "Um, wtf?!" She guesses the mass shooters and other dangers to society took the day off. It's the word kidnap for sure. Stay tuned for her new musical, Kimberlye & Rose Go On The Lam, coming soon to a theater near you!

Joseph R. Nunweiler-Meleka: A plethora of warnings.

1)Joe posted a picture or meme he found on Facebook of the Dallas Cowboy Cheerleaders dressed in Blue Handmaids Tales gowns. The meme said it was the "New Cowboy's Cheerleaders Outfits." Someone reported it as offensive and false, and it was removed. He was warned for posting something against the Facebook Nudity or Sexuality Standards.

Author's Thoughts: This again shows that the algorithm does not get humor and sarcasm and, I'm guessing, doesn't watch the Hulu show *The Handmaid's Tale*. "Blessed be, Facebook", " "under his eye." The algorithm is the Aunt Lydia of Facebook. Anyone that doesn't get that reference, watch the show!

2) Rhetorical Violence. Joe posted, "Who was it, I'll kick their ass for you" after someone posted something about a child being abused that included bruises. He was warned that it violated Facebook policies regarding violence against other people, and if he did it again, he would be banned from posting for a period of time. Joe said it didn't make sense because he was speaking rhetorically. He was pissed off because he didn't want to go to Facebook jail for speaking rhetorically.

He made a separate post regarding the incident and softened his comments. Instead of saying "kick their ass," he changed it to "beat their backside" and reminded everyone that a child abuser deserves everything they get, and he wished everyone a great day except child abusers. He wished them a sucky day.

Author's Thoughts: I'm surprised they allowed the word sucky or beat for that matter.

3) Joe also posted that he was watching *Shiny Happy People: Duggar Family Secrets* on Prime Video. His post said, "From a documentary standpoint, I think this is well done. From an opinion perspective, this family and their beliefs are completely F%cked. Absolutely disgusting Christian hypocrites." It got flagged, and he was warned that if he posted it, it might be removed or further actions may be taken because it went against Facebook Community Standards. He chose to post it anyway. As I write this book, he's not been arrested by the Facebook Po-Po. Joe said he was pissed because he thinks he has the right to voice his opinion.

Author's Thoughts: I honestly don't know how this guy got so many warnings without doing any time. I want his Facebook attorney.

Sudi Karatas

Sudi (a.k.a Rick), author of this book—for those not paying attention. My friend Katie Chin was doing a one-woman show in Minneapolis in May 2023, so I wanted to wish her luck. I wrote, "Knock em de@d," I intentionally didn't write the letter 'a' in the word dead so it would trick the algorithm and I wouldn't get flagged when it might misinterpret the expression and think I wanted her to kill her audience. Sure enough, a minute later, I got a warning that I might want to remove my comment as it might go against Community Standards. At least they didn't just put me in jail, which happened so many times before, without allowing me to remove a comment. So, I changed it to, "Knock 'em dre@d." So far, I'm still a free man. But a few people wrote on her page, "Break a leg," and I bet they are running from the Facebook Fuzz right now for promoting violence.

John Woods

John Posted, "Ban bigots, not books," and he was told it went against Community Standards.

The Crime's They are a Changin'

I read an article in USA Today by Jessica Guynn (Published 8 am Feb 23, updated 12:18 Feb 24) about Facebook giving more warnings before they lock people up. This is an excerpt from the article.

Tired of serving time in Facebook jail? You will now get warnings before being locked up.

Call it Facebook Jail reform. Facebook says it will now warn users when they run afoul of tis rules instead of taking away their posting privileges and tossing them in Facebook jail. For most violations, the first strike will result in a warning. If Facebook removes additional posts, users will lose access to some features. Facebook jail sentences will typically begin after the sixth strike. The old rules will still apply to more serious violations, such as terrorism or child exploitation, and offenders will face immediate restrictions, said Monika Bickert, vice president of content policy at Facebook parent company Meta Platforms.

What is Facebook jail? Why is it changing?

The shift to a more lenient approach is the result of feedback from around the world as well as the company's civil rights auditors and its Oversight Board, Bickert said.

"The one consistent refrain that we heard from those external groups was that they thought the penalty system needed to be fairer, more proportionate," Bickert told USA TODAY in an interview. Facebook polices billions of posts, photos, videos and comments each day. And, for years, its moderation systems have been slammed for missing context and bungling decisions.

Frustrated users complain they've been unfairly deprived of access to their accounts, communities and, in some cases, their businesses for days or weeks at a time.

"We started looking at the data and what became clear to us was that most people who violate our policies, they're well-intentioned people who either made mistakes, maybe they posted something close to the line and we actually made the wrong decision," she said. "There's a lot of room for education and explaining what our policies are."

Nearly 8 in 10 users with a low number of strikes did not violate Facebook's rules in the following 60 days, according to Facebook's research.

Author's Thoughts: Finally, in the months it took to write this book, it seems Facebook is at least starting to listen to people. One of my biggest complaints was no warning or chance to take something down. It still doesn't address the algorithm getting it wrong or users being unable to contact a human. Hopefully, this book will further show Meta/Facebook what they are putting innocent people through.

CHAPTER 6

Porn To Be Wild: Objectionable Material

In this chapter, I will expose the naked truth about how Facebook screws some people over by punishing them for posts Facebook claims have sexual content or are pornographic. Butt they are not. See what I did there?

Ken Howard (It's Not What it Looks Like, Literally)

Ken Howard, LCSW, CST, is a Psychotherapist, Coach, Sex Therapist Consultant. He's a nationally certified sex therapist through AASECT, the American Association of Sex Educators, Counselors, and Therapists, which is a rigorous credentialing program of hundreds of hours of training and supervised practice as a specialist form of psychotherapy. He is the founder of GayTherapyLA.com and has a private practice in psychotherapy and coaching based in West Hollywood, California. For many years, he has produced hundreds of blog articles and podcast episodes to support the mental health and well-being of gay men and gay male couples and polycules (a network of interconnected romantic relationships.) Back when he wrote more blog articles specifically on sex therapy topics, he promoted them with the 'boost' feature on Facebook Advertising. Without warning, Facebook banned him for life from both Facebook and Instagram from all advertising because their bots couldn't make a distinction between an academic, clinical article on sexual health and what they labeled as pornography.

He's also been banned numerous times as an LGBT activist for various phrasing. Once, he posted a photo of himself standing in front of a poster at the Los Angeles Music Center in downtown LA, where a production of Matthew Bourne's all-male Swan Lake was being staged. Behind him, the poster depicted a photo from the production of a shirtless male ballet dancer with large, white, fluffy shorts that ran from his waist to his knees, depicting the swans from the show. The second he posted the photo of him posing in front of the poster, Facebook instantly banned him for thirty days for pornographic material, even though the poster was displayed in the lobby of the Ahmanson Theatre!

Ken said, "Facebook tolerates Russian bots, white supremacists, Trump lies, Right-wing conspiracy theories, and all varieties of Right-wing crackpots, but, oh boy, try to educate on academic issues—He was an adjunct associate professor at USC for eight years, including teaching an LGBT course to graduate MSW students—or a poster from a night out, and watch out!" Ken believes it's appalling how much influence Facebook has, and it's derelict for the media not to expose Zuckerberg's ties to Trump.

Author's Thoughts: Facebook needs to be consistent and not hypocritical when it comes to weeding out those who really are posting pornography.

Blake Allwood: Hosta La Vista

Blake is the author of several gay romance novels, including *Another Chance, Romantic Rescue, and A Long Way Home.* Blake belongs to a gay gardener's group and enjoys looking at people's pictures of their gardens. Because he has been a gardener, he's often able to help diagnose issues. One summer, a man posted an image of his hostas, an eastern Asian plant cultivated in the West for its shade-tolerant foliage and loose clusters of tubular mauve or white flowers. He said he thought they had a fungus infection. Of course, the moment Blake saw them, he knew it was sunburn—hostas don't do well in full sun. So, he posted a comment that included a link to pictures of hostas that did have fungus and said, "See, this isn't what you've got. You're dealing with sunburn." Then he posted another link with pictures of sunburned hostas. Within seconds, Blake got a notification that his link had been tagged for pornography. What? Pornography? Hostas are porn? He immediately challenged the decision, and three seconds later, the bots got back to him saying, nope, the link to the hostas was indeed porn. He tried to fight it, but of course, there were no people to complain to. So, he was stuck for weeks in Facebook jail, unable to promote his books, unable to communicate with his groups, all because the bots think plants are porn.

Author's thoughts: Perhaps Blake's next book will be The Hostas Do Hollywood.

It's good that Facebook tries to weed out porn, the problem is this clearly was not porn which any human would know. Like many others, Blake's ability to promote his business, in this case his books, was shut down. A company that makes millions of dollars—In 2022, the revenue generated by Meta Platforms Inc., formerly known as Facebook Inc.. amounted to roughly 116.6 billion US dollars—should be able to hire people to search for smut on Facebook posts.

Peter Lancelotti: One Wrong Click

Peter is the author of *Alive After Dying* and *The Immortal Menagerie*. He has been kicked off Facebook four times. The first was for using humorous sarcasm, which the bots considered argumentative. The ban was for a day. The second time was another infraction of simple humor. However, this time, the ban was for a week.

The third time was his fault, he said. He was in a writer's group, and they were sharing a few pages of their stories. He's not into porn, however, a few days prior, he was watching a show called Supernatural, and he thought Jared Padalecki, who is on the show, was adorable. On a whim, he Googled nude photos of Jared and was shocked that it came up with several, including some of him with a full erection. Peter says he stupidly downloaded them but didn't check his clipboard. So, the writer's group said it was his turn to upload his pages. It was like watching a train wreck in slow motion as the most provocative photo of Jared slowly entered the screen. He tried stopping it, and just as it finished, he deleted it, but he immediately received a bot message saying he was banned for a month. The other writers were waiting for his pages. He had to private message all of them, which, of course, made him the laugh of the evening.

Another time he was banned was when a friend posted, "They ripped out tubes from my chest literally before releasing me from the hospital." Peter replied, "I hope you sucker-punched whoever did that. My heart goes out to you, Shane." He is a fan of Peter's author page and a friend on his personal page, so the guy knew he was joking, but Facebook said it went against its standards.

Trevor Augustino: Just Say No to Butt Crack

Trevor, who is retired and from Georgia, has been in Facebook jail seven times in three years. As long as sixty days and as short as forty-eight hours. He shared a friend's post and was censored, meanwhile, the friend's original post drew no concern. The most egregious ban was due to a post of his grandkids. After a day at the beach, they all came home, and Trevor was showering them outside. One of the pics showed the tiniest amount of butt crack. He was accused of promoting child pornography and jailed for sixty days. His employer saw his social media profile. He was fired two days later. He caters and hosts a food blog. Being banned affected the traffic on his pages, customer interaction, and his business, and he received a few negative reviews for being unable to respond. He tried to appeal and was told he had too many violations. He was threatened with a permanent ban if he received another infraction within sixty days.

Author's Thoughts: Multiple false violations are another problem. The violations add up like unpaid parking tickets, and each punishment gets harsher. If you could clear up the first wrong ones, you wouldn't have longer bans and restrictions on the other ones. Trevor lost his job because Facebook mistook or made accusations that were not accurate. I really think Facebook targets some people. How else can you explain sharing someone else's post, and you are the one who gets banned, but they don't?

Ken Stewart: Nasty

Ken, from Lawrence, Kansas, is an actor and a Massage Therapist who has been in Facebook jail probably about ten times for anywhere from twenty-four hours to seven days. He says generally, it's for his response to a story, once for referring to someone as white trash—if you saw the video, you'd understand. Another time was for saying that girls are nasty in fistfights after seeing a video where several teenage girls were in a street brawl and were tearing each other apart. The problem the algorithm had was the word nasty. It was crazy to him that a video showing horrible violence was okay, but the word nasty wasn't. He wasn't saying girls are nasty or that these girls were nasty. He was saying the way they fought was nasty.

He also posted a famous modeling photo of a nude Melania Trump he had seen on Facebook a hundred times but was told it violated Community Standards of nudity when he posted it. It was a joke during a discussion of inaugural gowns worn by past First Ladies.

Another picture that got him in trouble was of Britney Spears's husband in the gym with an outline of his penis showing. Again, this had been all over social media and posted by others after him. He said he sees bare butts all the time, but this image violated Community Standards. Please!

As far as how being banned or restricted affects or hurts him, he does business through Facebook and generally keeps it clean because of that. He was unable to do advertising and outreach. He tried to appeal every time and was stonewalled. Only once, when he posted a famous photo of Nureyev dancing in the nude for World Ballet Day, did Facebook reverse its decision. His appeal was that no genitalia was showing and that this photo was considered art and had been in galleries. Plus, the context was a famous dancer on World Ballet Day. They put the post back and let him out of jail, but he noticed it was still on his record. Ken also commented, "You guys crack me up," for a video on Instagram, and he was warned that his statement might go against Community Standards! It asked if he wanted to edit his comment. He didn't. He questioned, "What exactly was the problem?"

Author's Thoughts: Remind me not to post Janet Jackson's *Nasty* video on Facebook. That might cause a Meta malfunction. Ken pointed out that the crime he was cleared of is still on his record. That's another problem, when it's on the record, the next jail sentence you get is longer. It's not fair, but it's not called Fair Book, it's called Facebook.. I have some other words I call them, and some are included in George Carlin's comedy act.

Kerry Droll Refuses to Be Stripped of Her Rights for Non-Nude Pic

Kerry lives in California and was accused of posting pornography when she posted a picture of men in blue jeans, cowboy hats and boots, and no shirts. Facebook wanted her to delete the photo. She refused, and after eight months, they finally left her alone over the issue. She was accused again of posting pornography when she posted the link to her movie blog, and restrictions were imposed where she could read Facebook, but she couldn't comment or post. She says it's frustrating and insulting as hell when the Facebook bots pick out keywords and put you in Facebook jail without any humans bothering to review them before taking action. Yet, there are countless sites where Nazi groups post about harming people of color, Jewish, or LGBT people, and nothing happens. Their system is seriously broken.

Kefle J Callender: Don't Joke About Coke (cocaine)

Kefle is from Minneapolis, Minnesota, and is a huge Prince fan. His grandma used to babysit Prince when he was a child along with Prince's little sister. He's in the book *The Day I Was There* by Alison Howells Dimascio and Sue Houghton. His business, with partner Kitty Hopkins, The Great Purple Ride, is an intimate tour in Minneapolis as seen through the eyes of Prince. Kefle shared his stories with me.

Story 1

The year was 2021, and Kefle's friend Nicole took him to Florida for a week. She paid for everything. The roundtrip tickets and the hotel room. The hotel's name was Axel's, in South Beach, Florida. When they got there, he realized she had checked them into a gay hotel. He had no idea there were hotels designed for gay people. As they checked in, they saw the hotel advertising a pool party the next day. They went, and as he walked through the crowd, all the dudes were dressed in string bathing suits and having fun. As he continued, there was a group of guys smoking weed. Kefle was live on Facebook, showing all the activities. He approached the group and asked, "Does anybody have any cocaine?" He was kidding, but he was on Facebook Live, and as we know, Facebook doesn't have a sense of humor. He was put in Facebook Jail from May to September. He was like, "Daaayyyuuum, four months!". It hurt his touring business that he promoted on Facebook. He tried to appeal but was denied.

Story 2

Kefle went to this movie theater to watch Prince's concert, Sign O' The Times, on the big screen. As he watched, he took pictures with his phone to share with the people on Facebook. Well, there's the scene in the concert where Prince sings his song Hot Thing. He's standing center stage, and off to the right are three of his singers singing along with him. Two guys are standing on the outside, with the lady in the middle. Kefle posted that scene and got thrown in jail for thirty days because the algorithm thought she was naked, yet she was in a yellow two-piece swimsuit. Facebook said the picture was nudity and went against their standards. Well, Facebook, you are wrong because she wasn't naked at all.

Sadly, Kefle's page was hacked in August of 2023, and Facebook took his whole page down.

Author's Thoughts: The sad thing is if you're banned for pornography on Facebook, you don't get conjugal visits while in Facebook jail.

CHAPTER 7

Short and Sweet (Or Sour) Stories

This chapter includes long, detailed epic stories that go on and on. I'm kidding, or as Facebook would say, I'm spreading false information that goes against their community standards. I was being sarcastic, which I get to do in my book, unlike on Facebook.

Most of the stories in this chapter are shorter than Britany Spears' first marriage—and last marriage—but hopefully not as short as most people's attention spans. Where was I? I forgot, oh yeah, attention spans. Anyway, everyone likes a story that gets right to the point. So here we go.

Marie DeVivo from Arizona got into a fight with some girl on Facebook and called her a twat, and Facebook suspended her for calling her the 'T' word. She laughed it off. She filed an appeal, and Facebook responded that they have a no-tolerance policy for bullying, sexually suggestive content or hate speech.

Anonymous. Someone on Facebook sent me a message about his sister, who got a long sentence in Facebook jail for posting her dishes on Facebook marketplace. She made the mistake of titling her Facebook marketplace post "Fine China." The algorithm picked up the word China and, instead of taking it as dishes as intended, concluded it was an attack against the country and wanting them to be fined—possibly for unleashing Covid on the world.

Bonnie Vent is a Medium and spiritual artist known as the Spirit Advocate and the owner at Genesis Creations Entertainment. She was banned three times for oversharing her posts. She says she kinda thought sharing was part of the reason for being on Facebook. But she now sees that self-empowerment, peace, and togetherness are not favored on Facebook. They think it's spamming.

Robert Dalgleish shared a meme that Facebook said went against Community Standards. He was sentenced to thirty days in jail. The original post was still on Facebook. He thought he would test it out and reported it. He got a message saying that one didn't break Community Standards, yet it did when he posted the same post.

Shaun Wellsted, who is from the other side of the pond in Chesterfield, UK, had a friend coming over to his home, so he asked him to get him some fags, and he'd give him the money when he arrived. He got a thirty-day sentence. He tried to appeal, but according to Meta, he had used homophobic language. In the UK fags are cigarettes, so he didn't use a derogatory slur. Because he was banned and restricted, he couldn't write a birthday message to his daughter.

Author's Thoughts: The poor guy wasn't making anti-gay remarks. He just wanted something that might cause him lung cancer, so if anything, Facebook could have banned him for promoting suicide. I'm kidding, of course. When I heard the above story, I realized it was a good thing I didn't put my joke on Facebook about thinking of opening up a non–smoking gay bar in the UK with a sign that says, "No Fags Allowed."

Ted Burkow has been in Facebook jail many times for speaking his mind a bit freely in the comment section and getting an overreaction by some overly sensitive weenie—his words—that doesn't respect facts and several times for reposting images from other people's pages and groups to embellish his point. One that got him thrown in the Facebook clink was an image of George Floyd with the cop's knee on his neck. Another one was of a former Nazi officer because his lapel had the swastika. But he says the one that stands out the most was a Melania Trump post of her bi-sexual modeling photo shoots that are all over the internet available in any Google search.

Author's Thoughts: I guess Facebook was just trying to "Be Best" by prohibiting the Melania photos. Many people got put away in the Facebook slammer for posting that one.

Jerry Hensley got put in Facebook jail once for a post about the classic TV show Daniel Boone. He said his coonskin cap was the top-selling toy for boys and girls that year. They said it was a racist comment. He says anyone who knows him knows that he is not a racist at all.

James Mercel is a writer in California and has been in Facebook Jail about seven times, he thinks. He posted a picture of a guy in drag, as a mermaid in a wheelchair, wearing a fiberglass breastplate. They removed the picture for obscenity and banned him from posting for twenty-four hours. He appealed. They conceded. He did another twenty-four-hour stint when he responded to this exchange: "You're a duped, myopic, fascist, tw@t." Now, he uses "2@." The bots haven't flagged that yet. The 1st few times he was banned for something, he suffered withdrawals. After that, he just began to loathe Zuckerberg.

Ruth Davis posted on Facebook that she was once banned for an auto-correct when she wrote "Say no to tyranny," and it auto-corrected to say no to tranny's.

Kerry Droll. Somebody posted a photo of a huge spider and said, "What would you do?" Kerry replied, "Burn the house down." She was put in jail for thirty days for promoting violence. A few times, she received warnings of shutting her account down over memes Facebook said promoted self-harm. Of course, none of these things were true.

Jim Seeley. Facebook suggested some friends for him, and apparently, he sent too many friend requests in too short a time, or someone reported him. He got banned for three days without specific guidelines on how many friend requests are too many in a day or a week.

Tony Guadagnino was banned for twenty-four hours for liking too many pictures. His friend's twin brother died, and he posted about sixty photos of him. Tony liked them, and Facebook thought he was spamming. He got a warning and couldn't like anything for twenty-four hours.

Jason Bud is a fellow coworker and wise guy. Case in point, on the questionnaire I sent him, he wrote as an occupation that he is a public bathroom stall glory hole installation technician. He says he has been banned too many times to recall, but the one that sticks out is when he was banned for thirty days for posting this comment: "Faygo drinking jugalos blowing up clown balloon animals filled with helium, nitrous oxide and 'natural' gases at insane clown party concerts." Jason says, "Algorithms don't discriminate, and Mark Zuckerberg can sit on my FACEbook."

Author's Thought: I had to do a Facebook translation for Jason's answer. Translation: Birthday party clowns blowing up balloon animals."

Karla Guy responded to a post where Joe Biden talked about how rich folks did this and rich folks did that. Karla tried to post, "Wait a minute, Joe Biden is rich." A typo was her demise. It said Hoe instead of Joe. She got thirty days in the slammer.

Sudi Karatas. I posted a picture of the t-shirt I had made up. Marriage is 50/50. 50% a pain in the neck. 50% a pain in the ass! It said the post went against their Community Standards. Clearly, Facebook has no sense of humor. I put that slogan on a shirt on my Madlove Café site with other similar shirts at www.madlovecafe.com.

CHAPTER 8

How to Trick the Algorithm

As you've gathered by now, the Algorithm can be a real douchebag, pardon my Turkish. Some people have found ways of getting around it by using tricks. Most magicians don't give away their secrets, but in this chapter, we have a few stories of how some have pulled a Doug Henning on the algorithm.

KEYWORDS AND PHRASES THE ALGORITHM LOOKS FOR

Here is a small keyword list of things people have been put in Facebook Jail for when commenting or posting:

1) Men/Women are. . . will trigger a ban regardless of the term following. Do not describe men or women as anything.

2) White or the word trash combined with color descriptions.

3) Dumb...Sexual orientation. Do not add gay, lesbian, or trans to any post with a derogatory adjective. Also, Gay men/women are. . . In fact, any use of LGBTQ posts is grounds for getting a warning if put in a false light. The problem with this is that gays themselves are being banned for describing their gay friends as dumb.

4) Boys/Girls. . .Derogatory adjective.

5) Evil...Christians/Muslims/Hindus, or any religious organization.

6) Use of the word crazy goes against people with mental disorders. Even if describing your friend jokingly.

7) Anything with Covid-19 may spark a warning and flag for fake news or the use of the word Hydroxychloroquine.

8) The use of the word Nazi, especially in the context of photos of Nazis and other World War II posts. Mentioning Hitler will also cause a problem.

9) Calling someone a racist is a 50/50 split. You can be banned for the context or the use of the term. But the bot is indiscriminate.

Larry Heagle and his Bizarro World

Larry is an 81-year-old stand-up comic, singer-songwriter, recording artist, published writer, and author of the book *Not Really Sane, Not Really Sorry*, which I really enjoyed reading. What a life he's led. His Facebook crimes are far too many to mention. He says it took him a while to realize that Markie-Mark Zuckerberg uses algorithms to nab you using criminal language. Using the word Nazi or anything that in any way equates to Nazism will get your ass in prison faster than a lightning strike. Once, before he realized this, he had an Iowa friend who shares his birth date, April 15th. That also happens to be Adolf Hitler's birthday, so he posted, "Steve, all the great ones were born on April 15, you, me and Adolf Hitler." Bam! Back in Markie Mark's solitary.

One day, he came to the realization that in his profile description under Intro, he described himself like this: Cantankerous curmudgeon, a pariah. Alter Ego Bizarro Larry. If his followers were confused, all they would need to do is look up the definition of bizarro. Short for Bizarro-worldo. The opposite of the real world. Good is evil, round is square, and hello is goodbye. It was introduced in the Superman comics and used to extreme hilarity on a Seinfeld episode. After that? He has gotten away with Facebook murder by saying things like, "Bizarro Larry truly loves Mark Zuckerberg. He is the finest example of manhood, good looks, and generosity. Even his facial features are superb. He has a perfectly sized nose, diminutive ears and a wonderfully impish smile. He is, without a doubt, my hero of heroes." Bizarro Larry allows Larry Heagle to destroy politicians he says should be destroyed as well. However, one time he screwed up. He lives in Wisconsin, and they have Ron, or as Larry likes to refer to him, asswipe Johnson and Bizarro Larry should have posted, "I really love Senator Ron Johnson. He is without a doubt the most intelligent Senator the state has produced." Instead, he wrote something to the effect, "We need to hang his ass and remove him from office." Oops! For some reason Markie Mark only gave him a warning. "Hang" is a naughty hate word.

Because Larry is a live performer, he posted when and where he was performing so being banned put the kibosh on that. Now, he doesn't perform live nearly as much, and when he does, it is at prestigious venues that put up expansive advertising on their site. He says he doesn't really give a shit anymore. In fact, he finds it gives him time to do more important things than farting around on Facebook, which he does entirely too much anyway. He filed an appeal only once that he could recall, and the ruling went in his favor.

Author's Thoughts: Larry is one of the few who had an appeal go in his favor. He mentioned he used his ban to use his time more productively, so I guess some good can come of it. We do spend way too much time on social media when perhaps we could be out in the world doing more good instead. When you're banned or restricted, that's when you realize how addictive social media can be. At the same time, many use it to promote shows, books, movies, or things that can help others blocked from doing so while in a cellblock. Another lesson from

Larry is if you can find a way of talking in code like he did, you too can avoid some jail time, perhaps.

Innocent emoji trick

I saw a few examples of people posting innocent emojis to fool the algorithm. It's like the Rebus Puzzle game show that used to be on. Pictures are posted, and you have to sound them out to guess the saying. My Facebook friend Tony Guadagnino posts one every week on his page. Speaking of Facebook friends, that is one cool thing about Facebook.

Here are a couple of examples of the emoji trick.

Ho's Be Lyin'

Brittany Xen Osiris posted this on Facebook. She put a picture of a hose, a bee, and a lion. So, sounded out it said, "Ho's be Lyin." Very clever. If she had posted those words, she would have been banned. A picture is worth a thousand words, or sometimes it's worth a get out of Facebook Jail free card.

How to say cocksucker without saying cocksucker

Another post I saw somewhere said, "Congratulations!!! You're a..." and next to that was a picture of a rooster and a big colorful lollipop. Cocksucker.

The algorithm thinks it's so smart, but this is one way to fool it. You can also put asterisks and signal signs in place of certain letters. For example, b*&#h or F*%k or a$$h*le, etc. and most times you will get away with it. But not always. As I mentioned, when I spelled scum as "scuuum," that scumbag algorithm was on to me, and I got banned.

A Few more helpful tips on avoiding being banned.

1) Take a break in between posts.

2) Be careful tagging.

3) Never add anyone to a group without permission.

4) Don't post images from Google.

5) Don't use your account as your business account.

6) Like and comment at a normal pace.

7) Follow Facebook policy.

And to be 100 percent sure to avoid being put in Facebook Jail don't post at all.

CHAPTER 9

Do a Tribute, Get the Boot

Many impersonators and tribute acts are on Facebook, and that's where their audience is, how they let them know where they will be performing, updates, etc. Lately, Facebook has been taking down a lot of these pages, especially in the UK. The pages aren't doing anything wrong. They are not fakes or pretending to be celebrities. They are tribute acts.

Kelly O'Brien (Dolly Parton Tribute Act)

Kelly has been a Dolly Parton impersonator for fifteen years. It is her full-time job, or "9 to 5" job if you will, she's known as one of the best Dolly Tribute acts in the UK. She has even gotten approval from the Goddess herself through her cousin, who called Dolly, and Dolly said Kelly has her full support, she loves what she does. But now, she has been banned several times by Facebook. Meta, the parent company of Facebook and Instagram, shut the accounts of many musical tribute acts—via which many interact with fans, promote their work, and sell tickets—to try to quash identity theft and fraud. Again, Facebook starts with good intentions, and again, the innocent suffer.

I did a Zoom call with Kelly—couldn't find anyone to buy me a ticket to the UK to interview her in person—to ask her about her efforts to get her page back. She told me she thinks at least one hundred tribute acts she knows of have been taken down by Facebook.

Like everyone else, it is so hard to get through to anyone at Facebook, but she said Meta did start to pay attention when she started getting media coverage, including 4 TV News, The Daily Mail, Sky News, The Times, and some radio which led to her husband having an off the record conversation with the head of PR. They said they don't stop anyone from being on Facebook, and they told him, "We certainly don't take them down," her husband said to them, "But you are taking them down, and what comes up on the screen is, 'We believe you are in infringement of copyright and you are impersonating somebody.'"

Kelly says she doesn't believe Meta ever thought this would be a problem. They didn't realize how big Tribute acts are in the UK, where they take tributes extremely seriously. There are multiple theatres throughout the UK full of these tributes and impersonators. She said if you can't get the chance to see somebody perform, especially if they passed away, what's the next best thing? This is big business, and people spend lots of money on Facebook adverts.

Meta has created a monster, and we all use this platform because it's the only choice, no competitor, though she hears that they hate TikTok. In one of her interviews on TV, told them it's not like we can go to TikTok because she knew they wouldn't like that. You can't because the way it is set up is so different, and our demographic for Dolly, who is loved by people of all ages but especially over fifty, are only on Facebook. They don't really go on TikTok. So, while they are on Facebook catching up with family and friends and scrolling, they see something about the show and say, "Oh look at this, it's like a Dolly show, let's go see that". That's how tickets are sold now. So, when they take Kelly's page down, they take her livelihood away.

She said that every time you go to Meta Support, you get a different person—the fact she even got a person boggles my mind. She said probably if you have a business account, you can get through to somebody.

If you just have a personal account, kiss it goodbye. With a business account, you can add an admin to the account. So, let's say you add a spouse to it, and they take your account down, they can still have access. So that's some good advice from Kelly, to get a business account and an admin so it's harder for them to take it down. Then again, the juxtaposition is that her promoter, who helps sell her shows, is also sharing her business manager's page, so when her page goes down and gets banned, they sometimes lose access as well. It's never consistent. Luck of the draw. She said she gave the PR guy a list of names of other performers and impersonators, and he helped about twenty of them get their pages back.

She said it's soul-destroying, what Facebook is doing. You spend time and money. She told me the story of a woman whose brother had passed away, and his favorite song was Dolly's *Coat Of Many Colors*. She wanted Kelly to dedicate it to him in her show, and Kelly said she would. The woman told her which seats she was sitting in, and that day, Kelly's Facebook page got taken down, so she didn't know who she was and had no way to contact her because so much of the thread was kept in messenger or texts.

They are messing with people's livelihoods, but also there's a human connection. The reason Facebook started was to connect people, and what they're doing now is the opposite. They are promising something they can't deliver. Yes, there are certain people they need to keep away from Facebook. Pages that have a lot of damaging content. She thinks it might be a case of getting a human being to look at the site, and it would take a mere thirty seconds to find out if somebody is legit.

They are desperate to have you join Facebook, "Come, come join, create a page, join a great platform to connect people", which was great when it started. Now, people's accounts are being hacked. They're expanding. You can have several Facebook accounts, a business account, and an ad account when you get into business manager. It's like, wow, it's too much. It was better when it was simple, but it's growing like a fungus.

Author's thoughts: I agree with Kelly that they need to change the rules for Impersonators and Tribute acts. They need to change a lot of other rules too, because everyone is being affected negatively. Dolly's song *Baby I'm Burnin'* would probably be banned on Facebook for promoting and inciting pyromania, and her song *The Grass Is Blue* would be banned for spreading false information. Most of us joined Facebook to have fun. Facebook ruined the party, and if they keep it up, we'll have to go *Two Doors Down*—another Dolly song—for another party at a different social media network. Oh, I forgot, Facebook is a monopoly.

Kelly wants to spread the word and get Facebook to see the Light of a Clear Blue Morning—that's a Dolly song too. Kelly mentioned Meta has created a monster. I agree, and it's not called *Drinkinstein*, another rare Dolly song from the movie *Rhinestone*—Dolly has a song for everything, and I know them all. Kelly mentioned Facebook hates TikTok, which makes me want to use that more.

Vancie Vega: (Dolly Impersonator)

As an internationally recognized celebrity impersonator whose specialty is Dolly Parton,

The Not Dolly Show, Vancie's one-person show, is a completely immersive Dolly experience—a delight in celebration of the love for our Queen. The show features fan favorites and all the classic hits. This world-renowned Dolly Parton tribute has gotten praise from Dolly's family and friends. She had two Instagram accounts removed, but they have since been restored, thanks to Kelly O'Brien, who made it happen. Vancie received an apology from Meta for accidentally taking them down, and it was done.

Facebook post from a Dolly Impersonator fan

I came across this post from JDean Litner on Facebook about a Dolly tribute act.

I will say it again because I truly do NOT understand. Impersonators such as yourself make it clear you are not Dolly but putting on a tribute show while the scam artists literally claim to be Dolly and are very obviously running scams and Facebook says that is just fine. What these scam artists are doing is a crime but Facebook allows them free reign literally everywhere. It doesn't make sense in the slightest. Facebook is literally in full support of the scam artists while decent and legitimate acts are being punished. There's seriously something wrong with that.

Kerry Carlton-Senior CHERS Her Story

The owner of Carlton Entertainment & Event Management is one the UK's leading production and promotion companies specializing in Theatre production and Touring in the UK and abroad. It includes six touring theatre shows and tribute acts and concerts such as Tina Turner, Queens of Rock, Nearly Elton John, George Michael, Strong Enough UK Cher, and Celine My Heart Will Go On (Dion). Kerry is the Cher performer.

For some reason, the only page taken down several times is the Celine Dion one, the most popular show they do. It's odd because they post similar things on all the pages. One theory is a similar tribute show could be reporting it, bringing it to Facebook's attention, and maybe it's new Meta rules. They don't know. The page has been taken down and put back up eight times in six weeks.

In May 2023, they went on a popular morning TV show in the UK, along with Kelly O'Brien, who does Dolly, Carlton's Celine, and someone who does Brittany Spears. They did a performance and talked about it, and miraculously, the page returned the next day. The page went up and down another three times, so they sent a letter to Facebook. Their main issue is that they spent £45,000 promoting the page, every advert is approved, they have a review process so they know what they've been taking money for, and there's no way for them to get verification to stop it from happening again.

Yet Meta (Facebook) is still taking Kerry's money. Kerry sent a legal letter to Facebook, and she did get a very generic reply that said, "We've checked your page, and it's working again." But she says that doesn't stop it from happening again and doesn't put anything in place to prevent it.

Kerry and her company use it as their main platform to sell tickets for shows. No comfort that it won't happen again. She could spend another £50,000 in the next two years, and it could be taken down again. The Celine show has been running for two years and has 8000 followers. It's so unfair. They need to put something in place where you can be verified. If you're a business, how can they take your money and just shut you down? Strangely, it's the only one they have an issue with. Many of her friends, like Katy Ellis, the world's best Taylor Swift, and her Instagram—Facebook and Instagram are owned by the same company—are also having issues.

Kerry asked "What do we need to do to permanently fix this? They approve you again, but nothing has changed. They don't answer you." When her page went down, she said she had about one hundred phone calls and eighty emails back and forth with them, and every time, the same generic reply. She wondered if she was even speaking to a person. What do we need to do so it doesn't happen again? And they come back with, "You'll need to speak to this person" or "We'll forward your email," and she gets the same generic reply, round and round and round in circles.

Kelly's company also works in Spain, Lithuania, and some other places in Europe. The third time they were taken down, it took four weeks to get back up. The next time, it was back up in an hour. Maybe because she went straight to the legal department?

Chris Brown Tribute Act Theory

Chris Brown Tribute act, commented on Facebook in June 2023. I think it is a reaction to legislation. Countries have passed laws to make the online platforms partially liable for sharing content that risks infringing trademark or copyright protection. Their response it to take down anything that poses such a risk. Unfortunately, many tribute acts walk perilously close to breaking laws, including registered rights like trademark and unregistered rights like copyright or passing off.

The Intention May Be Good

Hayleigh Bosher, a senior lecturer in intellectual property law at Brunel University, says it's very sad that Facebook and other sites follow rules designed to protect artists. "From the perspective of the social media platform, they have to make sure they're upholding the rights of rights holders to avoid being sued themselves."

CHAPTER 10

Repeat Offenders: Multiple Infractions

"It's a badge of honor." Quote from many Facebook parolees.

So many people fit in this category—including me—of being banned and restricted many times. Depending on the crimes, many of them ended up in other chapters. But this chapter focuses on those who are real gluttons for punishment.

David Davis

David had one of his close calls in May 2023 when he got an alert on his Facebook screen as he was saving a post. It popped up saying, "Your content violates Facebook Community Standards. Your account has been restricted until Thursday at 6:13 am." He clicked the option "Disagree." About seven minutes later, he received an alert that said, "Your restriction has been reversed. Reason: your content does comply with Community Standards." He said it's nice when you can avoid a lengthy restriction by contesting it.

Here's a list of a few Facebook infractions David's had in the past, some of which resulted in jail terms. The first one, though, was immediately reversed.

1)In 2019, David posted a black and white photo of young Rue McClanahan holding an apple. Facebook detected a naked breast!

Author's Thoughts: Thinking the apple was a naked breast gives new meaning to the expression "How do you like them apples?" also, Blanche Devereaux would have probably been proud—Golden Girls fans will get that reference.

2) David posted a black and white image of Willie Aames on a Battle with the Network Stars post, which was flagged as nudity, even though he wore a Speedo. This one sent him to jail for a short term, but he definitely wasn't nude.

3)his *Cruising*—(the Al Pacino film)—post was flagged for a photo violating Community Standards. David thinks it had to do with a particular outfit someone was wearing in the background behind Al Pacino.

Author's Thoughts: To clear up any rumors, even though I've done a lot of background work in films and posted quite a few shirtless pics, it was not me in a skimpy outfit in the Al Pacino film that got David banned.

4) In 2019, a shot of Alec Baldwin from *Working Girl* was posted that violated nudity standards. David says his eyes really suck, and he didn't even realize there was a topless woman in the shot. It's the scene where Melanie Griffin's character walks in on Alec Baldwin's character in bed with another woman, and he says, "It's not what it looks like." Even though it was what it looked like.

5) The *Blue Lagoon* post from 2020 got him in trouble due to a picture of Brooke Shields and Christopher Atkins swimming naked underwater. Again, his eyes were bad, and he didn't notice that more things were visible than he realized.

6) David served a three-day Facebook jail term for his *Valley of the Dolls* post because of a certain word uttered by Neely, Jennifer, and Helen, included in the Quotes section. Even with quotation marks included, it was a violation.

David is sure there are more. He's being extra careful with pictures now. Anything remotely questionable, he'll discard because he doesn't want to risk another jail sentence. And when he reposts *Valley of The Dolls*, he always has to remember to edit that section of quoted dialogue.

It seems like Facebook bans some nudity and not others. They need to be consistent. David is lucky to have had any of these reversed. So many users get ignored and never get anywhere trying to resolve it. I don't know what David's secret is.

Ronald Rawson

Ronald is a Georgia resident, spending most of his time in Louisiana as a jet engine mechanic. He guesses he's been in Facebook Jail upwards of forty times. I wonder what the record is? He says he got banned once when he quoted Joe Biden. He got thirty days for jokingly calling someone a "lying dog-faced pony soldier." He got thirty days for posting a famous photo of some girls changing in the back of a New Orleans burlesque club. A nipple from seventy years ago was visible. He's been

banned multiple times for funny, sexually suggestive memes, and then
when Facebook sponsored an ad on his personal page showing a girl
giving head—an actual picture—he took a snapshot and posted it on
his page, complaining about Facebook's hypocrisy. He got thirty days
for posting the porn they had sponsored on his page.

He got another thirty-day ban for posting a picture of John Gotti.
The reason was he violated the dangerous persons standard, yet there
are dozens of pages about the Mafia, and John Gotti is all over them. He
found the same picture on another page and reported it for the same
reason. He was told it did not violate their standards. Another thirty
days for posting a picture of Hitler. No text or anything about him,
just an image. Same standard violation as the Gotti picture and, again,
all sorts of WWII pages and groups with zillions of Hitler pictures
in them. He had multiple bans for incitement of violence or bullying
when he was joking around with people in groups or making innocent
comments on a topic or news story. His most current ban was for
jokingly telling a friend that if he tried to take his beef jerky, he'd chop
his hand off. He says he got thirty days for arguing with a black woman
who was using racial slurs against members of a group. He doesn't recall
specifics, but it was things like "White bastard," and "White son of a
bitch." When he reported her comments, Facebook did nothing.

He said at first, being banned and restricted used to piss him off because of the arbitrary way they did it and their lack of taking things into
context. Now, it still pisses him off, but it's just an irritation. He said he
did try to appeal a few times. Every time he hit the "If you think this is
in error, let us know" button, he filled out the form and hit submit, and
he always got the message that something went wrong or their people
were too busy to take any further comments. He tried their oversight
board once, went through all the steps, and never heard anything back,
so he has never bothered with it again.

Author's thoughts: Ronald brought up racism and how a woman was using racial slurs. That may be a hard topic to distinguish sometimes. Most people don't think they are being racist. Sometimes, things are taken the wrong way. The issue, once again, is the lack of consistency with Facebook. While they should weed out racism or harmful, dangerous remarks, they need a system that is more effective in doing so. I have a character in the movie I wrote and produced with Tom Archdeacon, *Walk A Mile in My Pradas,* that when told to stop using homophobic slurs, the main character Tony, played by the late Nathaniel Marston, says, "I didn't slur, I said it very clearly." I probably couldn't post that joke on Facebook today.

Rob Garcia

Rob is the magazine owner and editor of a magazine called shift life design and has been in Facebook jail at least four times. The first time was when he jokingly wrote, "Don't make me carpet bomb you. I still know people." That got him locked up for a few days. He says, to be clear, despite being a former Air Force maintainer at the 11th Bomb Squadron at Barksdale Air Force Base, Rob does not own a B-52H model. He does not have access to live munitions and does not have the ability to fly one to conduct a bombing run within the continental United States. His next offense was a recurring post using a graphic of *The Jerky Boys.* They are prank phone callers from the 1990s. For some reason, Facebook labels them as obscene material, even a picture of them standing next to a pay phone. The most ridiculous one was when he wrote to a veteran friend who's a 'gun owning hardcore Republican' and jokingly said, "I'm going to get you tickets to a Nancy Pelosi fundraiser." He didn't threaten her, didn't write any bat crap political stuff, just that sentence. He got a thirty day ban from doing live Facebook posts, nine days of no regular posts, and a permanent ban on taking out ads.

The ultimate ban story? After all that crap, he named a weekly group Zoom call "Qanon meeting" and created a Facebook event. In eight seconds, everything he had was erased. Eight seconds. His Facebook personal account he'd had for a decade. His two Facebook business groups. His two Facebook personal pages. All erased like Marty McFly in that Polaroid—Gone. He had to recreate everything from scratch. It hurt his business for about a month, and he lost every online business contact. He tried to appeal numerous times and never got a response. He says Facebook has the worst customer service he has ever seen. They don't even have a customer service number.

Kathy Webby: Three Strikes You're Out

Kathy is a photographer and web designer who lives in New York. She wasn't playing softball when she got these three strikes against her.

1)A company-sponsored ad - One guy kept typing spam to anyone who responded. She responded positively for the company—she uses the product. The guy typed 'spam.' She typed 'troll.' Wham, she's put in Jail.

2)A friend showed a picture of a huge bee in her house, asking what it was. Kathy wrote: "Time to burn the house down." Jail again.

3)Kathy's son-in-law posted a picture of a poster in Washington DC that he photographed, which said something about 'time for women to take over.' Kathy said, "Some women politicians are just as crooked." Jail again.

Kathy was angry and fed up, and she lost business. She filed an appeal but never heard anything, and her restriction was not lifted for the thirty days specified. When she went to file an appeal for the second one, she gave up when she read the fine print. She doesn't remember the exact words, but it basically stated, 'We only choose a few appeals to consider.'

Author's Thoughts: It is discouraging to read that Facebook only considers a few appeals. And hardly anybody I've heard of gets their complaint read or the issue resolved. It's not just Facebook but most big businesses these days have horrible customer service. You cannot get through to a live person, which is so frustrating. Again, this is something Facebook needs to clean up otherwise, maybe there will be a Defund the Facebook police, movement!

Lito: Beethoven Rolling Over In His Grave

Lito, in California, is an actor, composer, filmmaker, and performing musician and has been in Facebook jail three times. The first time was for saying something about a horror film, describing a scene of violence to someone who asked about the content, to warn them about the graphic brutality. He guesses that for Facebook, trying to help someone only works if you don't use words that describe violent acts. He always appeals whatever ludicrous decision Facebook makes, but it never helps. They almost always stick with their initial decision. Except when they tried to issue a copyright violation for a video he posted that contained live performances of an orchestra he's performed with. They changed that decision once he explained that the recording was public domain, that his father recorded the actual video, and that Beethoven's music was not copyrighted. Of course, he also had to explain all that to them, which is ridiculous.

Lito also posted this on Facebook page in June of 2023:
"Facebook, your technology is trash. All I did was share a link to an exclusive article announcing the debut of the poster for OUR film. But, yeah, I guess that goes against "Community Standards". Bunch of idiots".

Lito says it hasn't really hurt him to be banned or restricted simply because he thinks he should be able to live without social media. Should, anyway.

Author's Thoughts: the fact that he had to explain Beethoven to them must mean Facebook is Da da da, Dumb, da da da, Dumb—sung to the melody of Beethoven's Fifth.

Matt Wolfe: 5x a Charm

Matt, a high school friend of mine, we went to the same college in Plattsburgh, New York, is a physical therapist assistant in New York and has been in Facebook jail five times. Once for calling a woman named Jane an ignorant slut. He says the Facebook Nazis never watched Saturday Night Live, where the news anchor always called Jane an ignorant slut. Another time he was saying that the neo-Nazis in Charlottesville, Virginia, should all be killed. He says the 'holy art thou nuns' at Facebook didn't approve.

He was also in jail for jokingly saying to a woman that she was a barren cunt. Oops. And another time, he posted a split picture of Michelle Obama and Melania Trump. Michelle was wearing a dress with no sleeves, and Melania was wearing nothing, from her porn days. The media lost it on Michelle but didn't say squat about Melania. So, Matt has done three days, ten days, two weeks, and thirty days. He said he's actually proud of himself.

He was put in jail in July of 2023 for another seven days. Someone had posed the question on their page, What book gives you strength and happiness? Most people said the Bible. Matt wrote, "You gotta be kidding me. Why read about orgies, killings, and polygamy?" He said, *Mein Kampf.* They said it went against their standards of hate speech. Oh well. Being banned didn't affect him other than preventing him from commenting on his friend's posts.

He said, "Fuck the establishment!" Tell us how you really feel, Matt. He never filed an appeal as he believes that shit only falls on the ears of Helen Keller and the conservative bitches that regulate Facebook.

Ed Reilly: Garbage In, Garbage Out

Ed Reilly is a Physician Assistant in New York. He also went to S.U.N.Y (State University Of New York) Plattsburgh with me and has had so many wrist slaps, bans, and accounts frozen and deleted over the years that he's lost count. He says most have been for calling out hateful people, the willfully ignorant, blatant racism, etc. He quickly figured out that you can't call people fucking idiots, scumbags or retarded. "Fair enough", he says. But he also found out saying things like, "You'll burn in your own personal Hell," and "Maybe one day COVID will kill someone you love," would be considered violent speech to the Facebook bots. As most of us know, asking for a review is a joke. No actual human ever reviews anything at Facebook.

He said, "Appeals are a joke. The boy don't understand sarcasm, parody, or even intent." With millions of people getting banned daily, having a human view your appeal is folly. Ed became a proficient seller on Facebook Marketplace and figured out that so many people out there want his garbage—yes, you can give away the things that would cost you extra for the garbage man to pick up. Recently, he permanently lost all selling privileges because he tried to sell a plastic pellet gun or an Airsoft gun. Little did he know they were considered firearms— immediate lifetime ban.

Author's Thoughts: I guess a pellet gun could put someone's eye out, but it's not a firearm. Facebook could have just told Ed to take that item down. If only laws and politicians were as strict with guns as Facebook is about posts about them.

CHAPTER 11

People Who Put Facebook in Jail

Many people have had enough of the corrupt Facebook Police force and have taken down their own pages.

Stella Parton

Stella is an accomplished, international award -winning singer and songwriter, a prolific actress, author, and a friend of mine. I enjoyed listening to her country hits as a kid on 1050 WHN. She had great hit songs like *I Wanna Hold You in My Dreams Tonight, Danger Of a Stranger, and Standard Lie Number One.* That last one went to number 1. She also wrote a tribute song back then for Olivia Newton-John called *Ode to Olivia,* coming to Olivia's defense when she won Best Country Female Artist and some Nashville people weren't happy about an outsider getting the award. I've enjoyed Stella's many CDs, including the 1995 *American Coal* and the one she did in 2018 called *Survivor.* And several in between including Resurrection, a dance album. She's been in over a dozen films including the Pure Flix movie *Nothing Is Impossible,* and did a great job in the TV movies *Coat of Many Colors* and *Christmas of Many Colors.* I also really enjoyed her book *Tell It Sister, Tell It!*

She used to be on Facebook but left and I asked her why. She said, "To be honest I was shocked by the hate filled comments by people on my page. Then totally stunned by how certain hate groups kept reporting me for my comments they didn't like." Stella was suspended for "violent content", and she never ever even thought of posting violence. Yet, she became continually disgusted by so many users on social media, she said, "That's the world we live in, if you disagree with someone, get your little hate group together and 'cancel' them." It's insane to her. But truthfully, she's happy not to participate on Facebook anymore. She is on Instagram and Threads, Twitter X, Tic Tok and has a YouTube Channel. Shortly after I spoke with Stella, she decided to go back on Facebook due to her fan base missing her on there. Her fans are delighted to have her back on.

Author's Thoughts: Stella isn't the only one to pay tribute and write a song for Olivia Newton-John. Olivia was one of my favorites, and in 2023, I wrote three songs in her honor, sung by Adrian Christian. The songs are, *Her Spirit Livs On, Through A Twist of Fate,* and *I Still Talk To Her Out Loud,* part of a whole Olivia tribute EP Adrian did. Available on all streaming services. All proceeds from the single *Her Spirit Livs On* we are donating to her foundation. The EP includes three Olivia covers sung by Adrian as well.

Vicki Wilerson

Vicki contacted me when she heard about my book and said I was welcome to share her story. Instead of Facebook banning her, she banned Facebook for a year because of all the censorship and vitriol. She voluntarily removed herself.

MY YEAR WITHOUT FACEBOOK

When Facebook first started, I was excited to sign up and use the social media platform. I was able to touch base with friends I hadn't seen in a very long time. It was new and fun. I remember one of my posts at the beginning was something about Facebook reminding me of kindergarten. People were kind to one another, clicking smiley faces on cute posts and giving a thumbs-up to everyone's comments.

Facebook, over the years, however, turned into something very different from its beginnings. It became a place where bullies would say the most horrendous things to people they called "friends" and to people they didn't even know. I was abhorred and mortified to see such behavior. People had started using it to ghost others and stalk acquaintances. Facebook had become a battleground for intolerance and divisiveness.

And that is one of the many reasons why I furtively left Facebook for over a year. And you know what? I didn't miss the medium One. Little. Bit. I did, however, miss some of my good friends and their positive, up-lifting and inspiring posts.

During the past year, I have had to care for some of the most special people in my life in a way that they had never needed before...and I was honored to do that...and I still am. In the little time I had left over, I learned some very valuable things during my year without Facebook.

I learned that a sense of peace had settled over me during my year of absence from the social media giant. Life was calmer, more serene. I was present—truly present—in everything I did. No more taking the time to write blurbs and post photos of my making wine, baking bread, having dinner with my precious husband, and camping with great friends. I did all those things, and I took some photos for my personal scrapbook, but I lost the desire to promote and gained the extra time it took to do it...and peace of mind in not having to monitor my account to respond to the people who took their precious time to make comments. And you know what? Most people didn't even care that I didn't post (we take our curated online selves too seriously sometimes).

After a while, I began to think of my dear friend, Henry David Thoreau, who said in Walden, "I wanted to live deep and suck out all the marrow of life." If life were the marrow, I discovered, Facebook was the fat. That "fat" had been, at times, unpalatable and always unnecessary, it seems.

My absence was a year that I grew closer to my husband and family. I stayed in touch with many friends though phone calls, visits, texts, lunches and camping trips. I somehow managed to still find out about important events in the lives of friends and extended family—just like before Facebook ever became Zuckerberg's entrepreneurial, maniacal, money-making monstrosity that it has become in so many people's lives. I didn't miss Mark and his greedy friends spying on my purchases and searches, only to shamelessly promote their advertising sponsors and cagy agendas. I got my information and news from independent sources, just like in the old days.

I lost no friends, no followers, no business, no money, no time, and no sleep. I still edited for other authors. I still wrote, and I lived a very full life, traveling, cooking, quilting, painting, crafting and sewing (and, yes, a tree does make a sound in the woods when it falls and no one is there to hear it, and people do live full, happy lives, even if they are not documented on social media). In short, I lost nothing without Facebook in my life. Facebook became...irrelevant. During that year, I was never ignored, hurt, insulted, gaslighted or excluded. I wasn't a part of any drama. Harmony and tranquility had been restored in my life.

As in so many cases, however, all good things must come to an end, and my time away from the social media behemoth has, as well. Authors— it seems—need social media (to some degree) in today's world. I have settled back in to editing a couple of novels that I had finished last year, so I suppose I need to inform my readers about releases and such. This time around, though, I will manage Facebook with boundaries (my new best friend) and on a calculated, scaled-back basis. I will operate with the knowledge that too much of a good thing is surely to become a bad thing, so I will release the unnecessary and will keep all the positive portions of what I have learned during My Year without Facebook.

So, who cares about My Year without Facebook? Perhaps, nobody will, or perhaps what I've learned may be beneficial to someone. If it is something that intrigues you, you might consider altering your presence on Facebook, as well. Either way, I wish you well...and peace.

Ryan Hathaway: Busted For Being A Wiseguy

Ryan set up two fake accounts, one named Nanny Pelosi and the other Donald Rump. He used stock images of each in their profile. When his friends posted about politics, he used the accounts to argue with them. He only used direct quotes from each of their real-life counterparts. It was comedy gold until he got busted by the Facebook Fuzz. Using direct quotes out of context took more time than he cared to admit, but the results were always beautiful. He even had the two characters get into a debate one time. He was dying thinking about his friends trying to figure out what the f#@% was going on. He thinks someone probably complained, and that's why they were taken down.

He finally got rid of his personal Facebook page, partly because Facebook closed his humorous fake accounts. He says people are way too eager to believe propaganda because it fits their personal political narrative. Seeing his liberal friends simp for big Pharma and his conservative friends overlook the Don's nonsense was just too much. He says his life is better without Facebook.

CHAPTER 12

LGBTQ Unfriendly: The Boys in The Banned Category

I'm not sure if Facebook restricts or is anti-LGBTQ, but some of its members and users are, and if they complain about something LGBTQ related and find it offensive, sometimes Facebook removes posts without doing due diligence. Here's an example.

Del Shores

Del is a writer, director, and friend of mine who I feature in my book *Rainbow Relatives*. Best known for writing and directing films such as *Sordid Lives, Sordid Wedding*, and *Southern Baptist Sissies*, he also wrote some episodes for *Queer as Folk*. He had one of his posts removed without explanation in 2014.

Del contacted Facebook three times but received no explanation. He wrote an open letter to Facebook asking what in his post did not follow Facebook Community Standards and why it was removed. The post was merely celebrating equal marriage rights in Pennsylvania in an episode of *Queer as Folk* that Shores had written several episodes for.

Another time, his page was blocked for thirty days after he posted a message about equal marriage. Shores uses social media to communicate with his fans. At the time, he had over 35,000 on his page. So, being blocked was a big deal. Shores said he doubts anyone at Facebook actually reads posts that are reported. He believes his pro-gay posts were being attacked by a homophobe, and he doesn't think Facebook did a thorough investigation.

Author's Thought: Maybe Facebook should hire Jack Smith—DOJ Special Council—he seems to do thorough investigations.

Shores suspected an angry reader encouraged many of his friends to complain to Facebook about the content of his page. He insisted there was not any obviously objectionable content—no nudity or outright hate speech. "I cannot believe that Facebook is homophobic. Otherwise, many of us would have been gone long ago," he said.

An article in Huff Post finally got Facebook's attention. A spokesman contacted Del to apologize for Facebook's error. They said that in an effort to quickly and efficiently process reports they receive, their community operations team reviews many reports. As you might expect, they occasionally make a mistake and block a piece of content they shouldn't have. They understand how people can be frustrated when, as in this case, a mistake happens. Del said, "The suspension was wrong! It was antigay. It was siding with religious nuts who troll my page daily, trying to silence me."

Author's thoughts: Del should copy and frame the apology he got from Facebook because it's so rare for them to offer one. It's even rarer than The Fonz saying he's s-s-sorry. In the words of Elton John, "Sorry seems to be the hardest word." Especially for Facebook. If Del had not been a celebrity and gotten all that media coverage, he would probably still be waiting for an apology today.

Will Kolb

Will is a Facebook friend and graphic designer in Texas who had a similar problem to that of his friend Del Shores with one of his thirty-eight Babylon groups—online communities he had on Facebook. I spoke with him briefly about his experience. Will had one of the first three groups on Facebook in 2009. He had several Babylon groups with 1 million followers. He got the nickname The Emperor of Facebook. One of the groups, Joan Crawford Babylon, was closed due to copyright issues over a Mommie Dearest post. His personal page was shut down once when he posted a picture of a male model, and one pubic hair was showing.

But the biggest issue was when his group Loud and Queer was shut down for weeks because of the title of the group. The algorithm probably flagged the word queer as homophobic, but Will says cutting gay content is homophobic. Facebook didn't understand the context or LGBTQ terms and lacked knowledge about anything LGBTQ. Loud and Queer doesn't offend, but he got a message from Facebook that said if, through the Babylon groups, he continued "this behavior," they would discontinue his personal Facebook account. He asked if there was anything he could do, but they never responded. They shut it down. He and Del Shores went after them together. When Facebook got bombarded by media people, it suddenly came back up. Will says he finally found someone who knew someone at Facebook, and maybe that helped, but he never heard from anyone—no comment, no apology.

Will says the biggest mistake Facebook has made is "There is no Human to speak to."

Author's Thoughts: The term queer used to be used as an insult, and it was offensive to call someone that. But the younger generation has taken back the word, and it no longer has that connotation. I must admit that word had such a negative meaning for so long it's hard for me to get used to it.

Peter Lancelotti

Peter was banned several times. Once was during a campaign on his author page after publishing his book *Alive After Dying*. He was using paid advertising on Facebook. Due to the controversial nature of his story on being gay and spiritually challenged, his page began attracting some good people and some not-so-good people. It seems that the not-so-good people felt the need to hit him with criticism based solely on his synopsis. He tried to be nice because he wanted them to attempt to see his point of view after hearing their vehemence.

Then, one morning, he checked his page. Unfortunately, he deleted it, so he doesn't remember the many Bible quotes the woman used. The gist of her missive was that he was going to hell for being homosexual. He distinctly remembers her saying, "I was once a homosexual," and she went on to say that she prayed the gay away. That did it for Peter. He started typing, "Congratulations on being able to quote the Bible! Did you stay up all night writing this?" Just as he was about to go on with his diatribe, Facebook notified him that he was being booted off for another month due to bullying. Bullying? Peter thought they had to be kidding him. The Algorithm cannot kid. It has no sense of humor. Shingles doesn't care, and the algorithm cares less.

Author's Thought: The woman said she prayed the gay away. Yeah, whatever. In my book *Rainbow Relatives*, about speaking to kids about LGBTQ families and friends, there's a chapter on religion called Pray the Gay Bashers Away.

I have noticed some of the Facebook jail pages contain a certain amount of hate towards LGBTQ and transgender people. Do they have a right to their opinion? Yeah, I guess, but if someone promotes hate, that should not be accepted.

CHAPTER 13

WTF Did I do?

"I promise not to do it again as long as you tell me what I did." This chapter is very short because if people don't know what they did, then there's really no story. It's usually just, "I got banned and restricted, and I don't know why." I almost left this chapter out and was going to have no chapter thirteen the way a hotel has no thirteenth floor, but here it is to prove I'm not superstitious.

Everyone loves a good mystery. Well, not everyone, but a lot of people. But not when it comes to being punished. You need to be told why. If you punished a child repeatedly but didn't tell them why, they wouldn't know what they were doing wrong and couldn't improve their behavior. In this case, Facebook is the child and must be reprimanded, and they definitely need to improve their behavior.

In the real world, you have the right to be read your rights and told what you are being charged with, not on Facebook. Half the time, people aren't even told why their post was taken down, which is so frustrating. The company sure does know how to enrage people. I call this Meta Madness.

Brad "The Dudeboy" Rogers

Brad, a journalist from California, says he's been in Facebook jail too many times to remember for the dumbest things, like jokes about Rednecks and Peckerwoods. Being that he has roots in West Virginia and comes from hillbilly stock, he figured that would be okay. When he posted photos of animals during wartime, he became a prisoner of Facebook again. The most interesting one was a WWII German soldier playing with a kitten. He has no idea why that was offensive.

Author's Thoughts: Perhaps the kitten complained to Facebook? Or he didn't sign a release form or was just being finicky as cats are.

The lamest reason Brad got busted was for posting some David Allen Coe lyrics—not even the dirty ones. The song came from a whole album of dirty songs the artist did, but the song Brad quoted was from *If That Ain't Country*, and the lyrics were, "The people who forgot about the poor white trash and if that ain't country, I'll kiss your ass." Several times, they did not cite the post. So, he wasn't sure why he was incarcerated. Being banned limited his contact with his friends. He appealed several times with no positive result.

Author's Thoughts: I think it was probably the term white trash that did him in. It's frustrating when you're not even told what's wrong with what you posted. I'm a big country music fan, so I like that Brad included a country songwriter in his story. David Allen Coe actually wrote one of my favorite songs that Tanya Tucker had a hit with in the 1970s, *Would You Lay with Me in a Field Of Stone*, which would probably get banned by Facebook for being pornographic because it has the word lay in it.

Alysia: Lack of Evidence

Alysia was restricted about ten times before the 2020 election over a nude photo she was never shown proof of, and she was not given the opportunity to dispute the allegations. She complained that what they had done was sexual harassment, and about a year later, the whole thing disappeared from the record.

Author's Thoughts: A year later? Yet another example of how slow justice is.

Jodi Fruchter Eisen: C.S. Cyber Security? More like B.S.

Jodi had some other run-ins with Facebook mentioned elsewhere in the book. But this one had her baffled. She got this warning in August 2023.

Community Standards

Cyber Security

x We don't allow people to try to gather sensitive information or share malicious software

x Encouraging someone to give away their password or username

x Using phishing or malicious software to get someone's log in information

So, she posted on her page.

I guess this is proof that anyone can lie about someone, and those lies can do horrible things. What Facebook just did to me is 100% illegal. Technically speaking, Facebook is cyberbullying me by claiming I did any cyber security violation. I spend almost every moment in my life helping to fight against cyber security crimes and other legal and identity theft issues. I'm glad I have lawyers and fraud investigators to help me get through this. I just pray that Facebook won't pull this crap with anyone else, especially someone who doesn't have access to quality legal and identity theft restoration help for a low monthly rate. Facebook violated its own rules—shame on them.

Author's Thought: I'm sensing Jodi was a little upset or angry. I wonder if someone hacked her and then tried to trick her friends into providing personal info. I guess Jodi can just call up Facebook, speak to someone, and straighten it out. Oh, wait, never mind.

Kerry Droll

Kerry was put in jail for thirty days for posting her Wordle score, just like everyone else did, and didn't get put in jail.

Rob Garcia

Rob was warned twice about spreading obscene and offensive sexual material and couldn't figure out why. That was one of his many trips to Facebook jail.

Author's Thoughts. Rob didn't even know why he was in jail for one of the bans, just that they said he posted obscene and offensive material but did not let him know exactly what. Facebook should at least let you know exactly what the offense is and what evidence they have.

That's it for this chapter. I told you it would be short.

CHAPTER 14

Capital Punishment: Pages taken down and executed.

This is the worst punishment Facebook dishes out. Deleting or shutting down whole accounts.

Everything is lost forever. Here are some stories from those who got the Facebook electric chair.

Jim Seeley Crime 3

A few years ago, Facebook deleted Jim's account. He appealed but was told they would not reconsider. They also told him they could not tell him why his account was deleted. He then wrote a snail mail letter to Facebook/Meta Headquarters in California at 1 Hacker Way, Menlo Park, CA 94025. Jim asked that, at the very least, he be told what he did wrong because he was planning to open a new profile and didn't want to make the same mistake again. About a week later, his profile was magically reinstated with no explanation.

 After much research and digging, Jim discovered he had been holding a multi-day friendly trivia contest with no prizes, cash or otherwise. A woman "frenemy" had it out for him and reported him. Apparently, only Facebook or their authorized advertisers can hold contests. She also reported him for other perceived transgressions, including posting pictures without attribution. He is not a professional journalist like her, so he didn't think the same standards applied to a private citizen. He said the three-day bans were no big deal, but having his account deleted was, in part because he had updated a lot of photos and then deleted them on his laptop and phone to free up space. For about ten days, he thought he would never see those photos again.

Author's Thoughts: It would freak me out if my account were deleted and I lost hundreds of pictures of family and events. If there were a fire in my home, I'd grab the cash first—all $20 of it—and then old photo albums on the shelf, things with sentimental value. Imagine Facebook wiping so much of that. Something money can't replace. Jim is one of the few who got his page restored, but there are probably thousands of innocent others who did not—shame on Facebook and their thoughtless actions.

Milo Shapiro

His website was "out of sight," literally

Milo is a friend who lives in San Diego, CA and is a public speaking skills coach. He's never been in Facebook jail but knows first-hand that algorithm of theirs caused a nightmare far worse and nearly impossible to resolve. One day, he mentioned something good that happened to his business and tried to end with the phrase, "Learn more at www.MiloShapiro.com!" He pressed enter, and Facebook said, "You cannot reference this website as it has been deemed to be outside of the standards of acceptance of appropriateness for Facebook" or something close. Milo was shocked. His website is about being a speaking coach, corporate team builder, and speaker using Improv games. How is that inappropriate? In what possible way? He has clients that range from ultra-liberal to hardline conservative, so he must, and does, have a squeaky-clean site.

He thought perhaps he could find a department at Facebook to either explain or override it. He did some digging, read blogs, and asked experts. He was continually told there was no way to talk to Facebook, and if that happened to your site, it was permanent. That's right, those of you who moan about two weeks when you can't post pictures of your dinner and cocktail, he was banned forever! And it's a big part of how he promotes his business.

He finally found a place where you could lodge a plea, but after detailing his problem and sending it, the confirmation note said that no one would reply, but his input would be considered by Facebook. So, begging for help was going into a virtual suggestion box. He hoped upon reading it, someone would reach out. Silly him. That doesn't happen.

After about a month of frustration, he contacted a tech expert, C J Gilbert, who is known for helping with unusual problems. CJ had not encountered it before but said he'd do research, too. He came back a few days later, saying there was a way to chat with a Facebook representative if you were having problems setting up paid ads for your account. Milo had considered that, but it wasn't the priority at the moment. He figured it may be a way to get Facebook to listen to a user. Milo tried the steps they described on the blog, but it didn't lead to the dialogue box shown in the steps. CJ tried the same steps, but he was able to reach the chat box. They tried it together, step-by-step, on Zoom, and could not determine why CJ could get there when Milo couldn't.

Their best guess was that CJ had been helping people with Facebook issues for a long time and had been grandfathered in for access, whereas Milo's newer sales login wasn't. In a chat session, CJ politely explained the issue, saying that his client—Milo—could not proceed with advertising because his site was unfairly blocked. Dave, on the other end, wrote back that an investigation would be made to see if his site truly failed to meet decency standards, and someone would let him know in three or four weeks. CJ and Milo tentatively booked a Zoom appointment with each other for six weeks out, assuming they'd hear nothing. They were correct.

At their scheduled Zoom appointment, CJ re-explained everything to chat host Pete, adding that they were still waiting six weeks out from the conversation with Dave. Pete asked CJ to hold. In under five minutes, Pete—or perhaps a supervisor—agreed that Facebook could see nothing wrong with Milo's site and that the hold should be lifted within the hour. To his shock and delight, in only five minutes, Milo could post about his site again. However, no apology was given, no credit given, no acknowledgment of three months that his site was innocently punished. Of course, he needed to pay the deserving CJ out of pocket. But more than anything else, it bothers him that he had to hire an expert, set up a business ad account, and plead his case twice. Facebook needs a simple appeal process where a business can say, "I believe you've misidentified my site." If they're afraid they'll be bombarded, they could even charge for the investigation with the understanding that the fee will be refunded if they agree the algorithm got it wrong. But giving no way to plead a case when Facebook is such a powerfully important medium is unfair. By the way, CJ has a great book called *Five Golden Keys To Sharpen Your Website.*

Robin Colucci

Robin interviewed me about my books *Rainbow Relatives - Real World Stories and Advice on How To Speak To Kids About LGBTQ Families and Friends,* and *How Catering Sucked The Life Right Out Of Me* for her podcast The Author's Corner.

When I told her I was writing this book, she mentioned that Facebook took her whole page down, so I interviewed her about that. This is her story.

She was having trouble logging in. She was scrolling on Facebook at 2 am, which no one should ever do. She got a message that said, "Someone has tried to log into your account from Taiwan. Was this you?" And she said no! Facebook told her okay, and they needed her to create a new password for security and asked her to enter her six-digit recovery code. She had no idea what a six-digit recovery code was. Apparently, Facebook has launched a new thing where you can create a recovery code. Ultimate paradox. She couldn't create a code unless she was logged in.

It said if that doesn't work, 'click here.' So, she did, and they said to be sure it's you, we need you to prove your identity. Please send us a photo of your passport or driver's license.

Now it's like 3 am, but she proved her identity, and they said they would let you back in—I guess released on her own recognizance. It started to open up, paused, and just as her profile started to come up, it shut down and said she was in violation of Facebook Community Standards, and was now banned from Facebook, and her profile was disabled.

She thought there must be some kind of customer service contact— by now, the reader knows this is not the case. She had her operations manager research how to get through to someone. None was found. She then asked her manager to read the entire Facebook Community Standards, and she had not violated any of them. She was never able to get in again.

She did finally realize part of what happened. She was working with a podcasting company that posted her podcast on their page on her behalf, which does not violate Community Standards—she checked. As far as she knew, all their employees were in the Philippines, so when she got a message that someone was trying to post from Taiwan, she didn't realize it was probably the podcast company that neglected to tell her they'd added an employee from Taiwan. Regardless, she did not violate any of their stated Community Standards. She doesn't believe she was hacked. To this day, she is not back on Facebook.

She shared some of the impacts. It's so irresponsible on Facebook's part and hugely problematic. She believes the U.S. Constitution has some very clear guidelines for what constitutes a violation of any law. Usually, you are required, if you are going to take away privileges from someone, to tell them precisely what they did wrong and allow them to communicate their side. This never happened. She was given no due process. Put in jail without cause and summarily executed without any chance at redress. It caused her other problems as well. She wanted to change the name of her Instagram account, which she can't do because she needs to log in to her Facebook account first. She also has a business page on Facebook where she was the only admin, and she hasn't been able to do anything for over a year. As far as the Facebook community is concerned, she's abandoned her business and has no way of taking it down.

She feels this is gross mismanagement of a social media platform. It's potentially undermining her reputation. There's no one to contact. She and her assistant scoured the internet for ways they might be able to. She did find one email address where she sent a very long email outlining everything that happened, asking for help, and even pointing out she's a small stakeholder in the company. The email bounced, saying it had been returned because the mailbox was full.

Author's Thought: Of course, the mailbox was full, thousands of people are having issues, and no one is checking the emails.

Robin said she understands it's a wonderful power to have millions of customers, but it's also a responsibility, and they are not living up to it. When she considers Mr. Zuckerberg's plans for Metaverse, she's even more concerned for the well-being and welfare of its users—which she will not be. If a person invests in Metaverse at the level Mr. Zuckerberg hopes they will, some will probably be very vulnerable and have put a lot of money into building this phony life in the Metaverse. If those policies persist in putting people out in the cold and killing them off without any chance to be heard, she fears the Metaverse could become the source of many suicides and other negative outcomes for people who are vulnerable and lonely.

Robin knows how it feels, it was an adjustment for her being banned. She didn't spend a lot of time on there but did use it as a way to keep in touch with people. It feels very isolating. She cautions anyone considering participating in the Metaverse that she thinks you're entering very dangerous ground, and this guy can rip you off for thousands of dollars. She had fifteen years of memories, photos, posts she didn't have anywhere else, significant events she shared with people, received condolences, whatever. And they are gone forever.

She is on LinkedIn—They actually have customer service!

CHAPTER 15

Fake Accounts, Hackers, and Bots, Oh My!

Many celebrities have this issue of people pretending to be them, including one of my favorite country singers, Tanya Tucker. Shirley Ruehle, who runs the Facebook page Tanya Tucker People Only, that has over 50K members, has to keep warning members to watch out for all the Fake Tanya's, the scammers. The real criminals are dealt with much later or not at all, while the legitimate ones, such as tribute acts pages, are taken down.

Another issue is that many users' accounts get hacked, and the perpetrators seem to get away with it. The expression that comes to mind is, "Where's a policeman when you need one?" Same with the Facebook police. They aren't around to catch the hackers but have plenty of time to lock up law-abiding cyber citizens.

Gary Curtis Mitchell: Panama Prison

Gary lives alone in a jungle paradise in Bocas del Toro, Panama, which is only accessible by water. His boat had been inoperable for nearly a year, so he depends on his wonderful neighbors to take him to the store once a week. He owns Green Acres Chocolate Farm and Botanical Gardens and is the Executive Director of the Environmental Nonprofit Planet Rehab. He uses Facebook for friendship, business communication with members of Planet Rehab, and, most importantly, emergencies!

In Panama, it is his experience that Facebook is the primary source of communication. He received a Facebook message stating that his business page for Green Acres was at risk of being shut down for violating Facebook Community Standards. That confused him because his business page is meticulous about what's posted. While he was verifying that he was indeed the Facebook contact for Green Acres, he received another message that his personal Facebook account was in violation by posting—disgusting nude pics—against Facebook Community Standards. Facebook suggested that perhaps his account had been hacked and suggested he change his password. While changing his password, Facebook suspended his account for several days. For him, that had genuine real-world consequences.

1). He lost business. He could view messages from people who wanted to schedule a tour, but Facebook did not let him respond.

2). He lost communication with his nonprofit group when he had a planned event.

3). A snake that he couldn't immediately I.D. entered his living quarters, killed one of his birds, and threatened another. He is a member of several Snake I.D. groups that respond almost instantaneously when he uploads a picture of a snake he can't I.D.

This entire situation left him angry, upset, lonely, and generally bummed out. He's at a loss as to why someone would hack his accounts for the sole purpose of posting inappropriate pictures. And he is quite disturbed at how Facebook is set up to handle or handle badly, that sort of issue. He is the victim of a hacker, and while Facebook suggests he may have been hacked, they simultaneously ban him for three days. For many, especially in the US, Facebook is just a fun social tool. For Gary, where he lives, and probably many others, Facebook is crucial.

BAMBOOZLING THE BOTS

Using automation tools or bots to create fake engagement on your posts is strongly prohibited by Facebook. Moreover, Facebook does not allow you to use a bot to send messages to anyone. In addition, it is also against Facebook's Community Standards to use automation tools to send friend requests. If you violate any of these, your Facebook account will be banned.

I get messages from Bots all the time. Facebook does not seem to enforce this rule at all! On many of my posts and other people's, a bot will like and post a message, saying they want to be your friend and tried to send a friend request, but for some reason, it didn't go through, so please friend them—or something to that effect. The grammar is always bad, it's overly complementary, and it's obvious it's fake, but some people probably fall for it. I reported many to Facebook, but they said they found nothing wrong with those pages. Unbelievable. Being the wiseass that I am, I started having fun with a few of them and engaging in a "fake" conversation just because I like being sarcastic. This is one example. It's a fun game. This was the conversation I had with one of them.

THEM—Sandra Tony. Rick Sudi Karatas You have a very nice and lovely post.

I was actually searching for a friend of mine then came across your handsome profile post.

I have no choice but to say hi to you. You are a very handsome man especially with those handsome smiles on your face I already tried to add you but I couldn't, I really want us to be friends, can you add me. Thanks you so very much.

ME: Sandra Tony, those handsome smiles are from gas. Before I can add you as a friend, I need you to answer this question: what did I have for breakfast three weeks ago?

THEM: Rick Sudi Karatas, it honest with you I am not in magician so I don't even know. Can you please add me up so we can change ideas and get to know more about ourself.

ME: Sandra Tony, I will try to add you up but what numbers do I start with?

THEM: Rick Sudi Karatas you are a very funny guy and you look cute but just add me up on Facebook.

ME: Sandra Tony, why do you have two first names? Also, can you pass the ketchup then I will add you up once I find my calculator.

Another Conversation:

THEM—Mia Wilson: Your posts are always worth reading, but we are not friends on Facebook, I sent you a friend request but it didn't go through, if you don't mind adding me as a friend on your Facebook, hope I get it soon, thanks for your letter

ME : Mia Wilson, will you marry me? I need a green card.

MIA: What◈

ME: Well? Shall we tie the knot?

No response

ME: I feel we know each other well enough to get married but just a heads up...I want to have ten children...Some twins and triplets would be okay if you don't want to get pregnant that many times.

She had stopped responding to me, but I kept going. Bots, like my family, get tired of my humor.

And One More:

Alice: Your post is very interesting, you share a lot of things in life and know how to share, it's something everyone needs to stop and think about, nice to meet you, please add me as a friend

ME: Alice Arion, sorry Alice but you don't live here anymore but come back and ask me when you're ten feet tall

Alice: Rick Sudi Karatas Haha, you are so interesting. I see you have so many friends list. Do you also like to meet new friends?

ME: Alice Arion, no

Last One:

Christina: Can you add me as a friend? You are recommended by Facebook (a friend you may know). I look forward to your reply. I wish you all the best!

Me: Christina Wilson I wish me all the best too.

Christina: Rick Sudi Karatas, ok can you add me up and let's chat.

Me: Christina Wilson, I added you up....0 plus 0 = 0.

Christina: Rick Sudi Karatas, how are you doing today.

Me: Christina Wilson, I'm okay but my menu options have changed.

Christina: Rick Sudi Karatas, okay well nice to meet you here.

Me: Christina Wilson I wish I felt the same.

Christina: Rick Sudi Karatas, where are you from and how is the weather over there now.

Me: Christina Wilson, I am from the planet Xanadu where the temperature is always 69 degrees and it's always windy with tornadoes 34 times a year

Hackers targeting Facebook pages of animal rescue organizations.
Saw this on Facebook by, Mallory Sofastaii
Posted at 3:36 PM, Jun 29, 2023 and last updated 3:31 PM, Jun 29, 2023

BALTIMORE. Animal rescue groups are being targeted by hackers on Facebook. Their pages are taken over then used to solicit money from unsuspecting donors. These rescue organizations rely on their social media accounts to fundraise, adopt out animals, and reunite lost pets with their owners, but when their pages are hijacked, their life-saving missions are stalled, and they said they've received little help from Facebook.

Recent Stories from wmar2news.com

"She was running as a stray in Parkville and I took her in," said Leah Biddinger, president & founder of Bring 'Em Home Animal Rescue and Trapping. Biddinger found Marshmallow, a three-year-old Pitbull mix, on the street. She believes she was used for breeding and in an abusive home. She brought her in through her rescue and found her a loving home, until that owner became sick. Biddinger is now searching for Marshmallow's forever home, but it's been a struggle after she lost access to her rescue's Facebook account. "It was on May 17," said Biddinger. "I went to my Facebook page for the rescue and found that I couldn't access it.". Someone locked her out then used her page to post fake puppies for sale.

Non-profits say Facebook was unresponsive to their pleas for help.

Author's Thoughts: Of course they were unresponsive! It's Facebook!

CHAPTER 16

The Verdict: Facebook
GUILTY!

They have punished so many innocent people. They are guilty of hypocrisy, absurdity, a lack of common sense, and being too cheap to hire real people to sort out the mess the algorithms have created.

Facebook Crime: Inconsistency

Facebook is not consistent with banning and restricting. It's good Facebook tries to avoid spammers, but again, it's usually the innocent ones who get punished while the real spammers run amok.

Jodi Fruchter Eisen: Green Eggs and Spam

Jodi reported fifty scammers, and Facebook said there were no violations. She reported racial and hateful comments that Facebook allowed to stay. One time, shortly after having cremated her daughter, she reposted a video of a child's funeral with a comment stating something like, "The worst thing that could ever possibly happen to a parent." She was banned for a month despite a letter she wrote explaining why she reposted it. Sometime after that, she saw a darling little video of a cute little dog running around carrying a large branch in his mouth. She thought it was absolutely adorable, but Facebook said something about it being dangerous—too long ago. She doesn't remember the exact wording. Jodi says she doesn't know why they ignore hate and violence posts but ban stuff like that. The ban hurt her because she was unable to find out about people she cared about and was not able to promote her business, and like many others, her appeals fell on deaf ears.

Facebook Crime: It Has No Sense of Humor.

Big debate: should we be able to joke about anything? Can jokes be taken too far? Should certain jokes not be allowed? I like to joke and write comedic sketches and scripts, and if we restrict that too much, comedy will suffer. Freedom of speech will suffer. It's good that Facebook doesn't want people to bully others, but half the time, friends are just joking amongst themselves, and an algorithm eavesdrops and decides you need to be punished.

Facebook Crime: Guilty of exceeding the Statute of limitations

Facebook users are sometimes punished for posts from years ago that pop up as memories. Things posted before it even violated a Community Standard. Here are two examples.

Joseph R Nunwieler-Melek: Bleach your Children Well

In April 2020, Trump suggested injecting bleach to get rid of Covid-19. There was a funny meme going around on Facebook showing a working-class guy on his back with his butt above his head, with a bottle of bleach like he was pouring it in his butt. The meme said, "Am I doing it right, Mr. Trump?" Joe thought it was funny, so he posted it.

The picture was there for at least two years, and then out of nowhere, he gets a notification that a picture he posted was removed for violating Facebook Nudity or Sexual standards, and if he keeps it up, he will be banned.

He was shocked because the picture had been on Facebook for a couple of years, and he got the original picture from Facebook in the first place.

Author's Thoughts: During that whole bleach thing, I made a meme of my own with a picture of the *I Love Lucy* episode where Lucy does a commercial for Vitavitavegimin. In the picture, she's holding up the bottle. In the meme, instead of Vitavitavegimin, I wrote, "**Ivermectin**vegiman, tastes just like candy". Ivermectin was being recommended by certain individuals along with Clorox to fight Covid-19. I'm surprised I didn't get banned for posting it.

Danny Rafferty (Dj Riff Raff): Another Clorox Controversy

He's been in Facebook jail twice. He posted a meme back when Trump was in office, and after he had suggested injecting bleach as a cure for Covid-19, a meme popped up of Clorox Chewables. He posted it in 2020 or 2021. Facebook gives you daily memories, and he got busted for something he had posted a year prior. The second time he ended up in Facebook Jail was for sharing a meme he had posted years ago at Thanksgiving, and it popped up on Facebook memories, so he shared it. It was a meme of Jeffrey Dahmer, and it said, "No one is going to tell me how many people I can have for dinner on Thanksgiving." In both incidents, they said, "Did we get this wrong?" he tried to appeal their decision and said, yes, they got it wrong, and both times, they came back with, "We confirmed your post didn't follow the Community Standards."

Danny said they gave him a thirty-day sentence in both cases, but when he tried to appeal them, they ruled against him and doubled the sentence to sixty days. Once they rule, there's no way to contact them to continue fighting it. It's so unfair, he said. Where is his right to face his accuser? They give you no trial, nothing. You have to accept their ruling. He said it affected him in that it caused him emotional distress from not being able to appeal the case further and not being able to communicate with anyone about it. He couldn't go live on Facebook. The first time he went live was as a college student in Radio and Television, and not being able to go live interfered with his schooling in the last months just before graduation. He says they don't give you any way to appeal it once they rule against you.

Author's Thoughts: I've come to believe that when Facebook asks, "Did we get this wrong?" it is a rhetorical question. Also, being unable to appeal on Facebook makes Facebook less appealing.

Facebook Crime: Mishandling of copyright material evidence

Again, Facebook is not consistent. They punish or lock up certain people who post material they have permission to use or belongs to the one who posted it, while thousands of others post plenty of copyright material and get away with it.

Patrik Simpson: Facebook Wrong About Copyright

Patrik got in trouble with the Facebook Fuzz when he and Pol Atteu attended The Michael Jackson Estate Halloween Party, which they attend every year. The estate is closed, and they do a Thriller party with dead Michael Jackson zombies walking around. His kids, Prince, Blanket, Paris, and nephews, hosted the party.

Last year, after the event, the hosts sent a video to Patrik and all the guests who attended the event with a recap. Michael Jackson's Thriller music is in it. Patrik posted it on Facebook, and he was banned and blocked. They said he was using copywritten music without authorization. He sent them a screenshot of the estate, saying he had the right to use the music. Patrik was an invited guest at the party. The hosts were the ones who sent him the video with Michael's music. Facebook denied the claim, but Patrik was told he could file an appeal. So he did with the screenshot from the email, and he was able to log back in after seventy-two hours, however, it took thirty days to get the appeal of the music back, which he finally did. Patrik and Pol do a lot of promoting things for their business on Facebook, so being banned and restricted is a big pain in the neck—and other parts of the body.

Walter Stanley: An Innocent Man Kept in Jail

Walter wants to know why he spent thirty days in Facebook jail. The charges got reversed, and it was no longer a violation, yet he still spent thirty days in Facebook jail with no one to go to about fixing it. He wants time credited for time served. "You're here, technically not in jail. You're home with an ankle bracelet."

THOUGHTS FROM AUTHOR BLAKE ALLWOOD

"It feels like over time, Facebook has made so many changes, and few, if any of them work in the interest of its customers. For example, when I first started my business as a writer in 2019, Facebook was one of the most important elements of my business. I'd put information about a book I was writing out, and people could see and access that information readily.

Then groups began to take over, and even there, I was able to build a strong audience for my books. In fact, the first summer I had my group, in 2020, we had a Pride event that hundreds of people attended—online—and was highly effective.

Then something changed in the groups as well. Facebook shifted things so that only certain group posts were seen. Then, it became almost useless to do big events like the Pride event.

After Zuckerberg testified in Congress in 2021, it seemed like things changed fast. Bots began to ban people left and right. Of course, at first, I thought this was good because, during the 2020 election, Facebook posts were over the top with ridiculous lies and misinformation. However, now it's clear the bots are designed just to do a wide sweep with no effort to weigh the nuances of communication. For me, and I admit I'm nowhere near the back scenes of Meta/Facebook, it seems there is no thought behind the changes. And if there is thought, it is based on whatever whim Facebook has at the moment. I honestly can't see where Facebook is considering its users. Even as an advertiser who should be one of the most important people for the Facebook business, I don't think the organization cares about my needs.

If it's true and Facebook is flowing at its own whims, it is unfortunately headed toward a deep and ugly crash because no matter how powerful you are, ultimately, if you piss off the people who use you to the point that they are more frustrated with a product than they enjoy it, there's no way that product will survive."

Blake also has thoughts on the nuances of social interaction.

"I think it's important, especially as we look at content, that words have different meanings for different cultures. It's also important to realize that for groups who have been treated unfairly or with extreme aggression, certain words used by those cultures are intentionally done to take the impact and power away from such words. Social anthropologists often discuss

this in regard to cultural groups, such as the black community, using the N-word. The gay community using Fag or calling themselves Girl or even Bitch. Those comments have been used to undermine and even violently destroy people, so naturally, those groups have a fundamental right to use them to empower themselves. When bots are in charge of Facebook inter-actions, with no possibility of human appeal, that negates the freedom so desperately needed by disenfranchised groups. Naturally, this is some-thing that concerns a lot of social anthropologists and cultural leaders alike. Ultimately, organizations run by one cultural group shouldn't be controlling the dialogue of minorities. The way Facebook's bot system is currently set up, that's exactly what's happening."

POLITICS, RELIGION AND SEX

Don't talk in public about politics, religion or sex is a rule we've been hearing for years, but it's even truer on Facebook. Most arguments and banter back and forth come about from discussions on these subjects. Especially with politics, you're not going to change anyone's mind, yet people will spend hours going down the rabbit hole trying to convince someone else what is right. I must admit I am guilty of this myself. It can be fun and frustrating at the same time, but definitely a waste of time.

Part of the problem is that so much misinformation is being allowed out there. It is so hard to know what is true that it's hard to discuss any-thing when no one has the facts. At least Facebook was trying to stop false information about Covid-19 because it can be dangerous if people are told something that may harm them. Spreading false information goes against their standards, but who decides what information is false?

Even though you are not supposed to talk about politics and are asking for trouble when you post something political, I wanted to include the following story, which is political, but I can really see his point of view.

Carlos Moreno Jr doesn't want to be an American Idiot

Carlos is an actor in L.A. During the 2016 Presidential Election, he was very engaged on Facebook, as many others were. When Trump called Carlos' heritage—Mexican—rapists, murderers and drug dealers, he took it personally and quickly went on social media to say that if Trump did that to divide us, we were on a path to the destruction of our democracy. Carlos felt demonized by a presidential candidate, and people seemed okay with that. He lost several family members due to Trump and his divisive rhetoric. He went on Facebook and stated his reason for fighting Trump pointing out that there are rapists, murderers and drug dealers in every ethnicity, but many on Facebook just wanted the fight. Carlos started a heated debate with a few hateful people, and he says he should have known back then, "You can't debate stupidity or a rock." He mentioned in one of his responses that he didn't want to be like what Green Day sang, 'An American Idiot.' That got him banned for about ten days because he broke their rules.

The president was allowed to break the rules, but Carlos was in Facebook jail. All for criticizing the nominee? Eventually, Trump got barred from Facebook, but it was after a few people died on January 6, 2021, during the insurrection that a former president encouraged. He stopped using Facebook throughout Trump's administration for fear of retribution, and currently, he uses it only to promote his work. It took one man to ruin his positive outlook on social media. Carlos says he was only doing what Trump was doing. He wouldn't have had a problem with it if Trump and his minions had also received the same treatment. Carlos couldn't defend himself from Trump or others who bullied him. He says Trump still can't shut up. If his mouth is moving, that means he is lying and still spreading hate.

Author's Closing Thoughts: There are so few choices regarding social media outlets. I found a few others, but none of those networks have come close to Facebook's number of users. I almost wish MySpace would come back. I liked that platform. Maybe I'll start a social network called OurSpace, which sounds more inclusive. Hopefully, thanks to all those who contributed stories for this book, Facebook will take some action towards fixing these issues. I'm not holding my breath, though.

ACKNOWLEDGEMENTS

I would like to thank all those who gave me their stories of their incarcerations and run-ins with Facebook Fascists. Thanks to Tim Heagerty of Heagerty Design

for doing an awesome book cover. Ironically, he was banned from "social media" messaging because we discussed the book cover on Facebook.

Thanks to my partner Carlos Romani for taking the cover picture and supporting all my projects.

Larry Weissman for taking the back cover author photo.

Stella Parton for her friendship and her story in the book.

Special thanks to Blake Allwood for his help, advice, and the thoughts he shared in the book.

Thanks to Jo Bird for editing the book.

And thanks to Mark Zuckerberg, if not for him opening up his prison, there would be no book.

REFERENCES AND RESOURCES

RESOURCES

Websites of people and businesses mentioned in the book
C J Gilbert,
 http://www.gilbertstudios.com,

Ken Howard
https://gaytherapyla.com

Robin Colucci/The Author's Corner
https://theauthorscorner.com/

Vancie Vega

https://www.facebook.com/vancievega/about
http://www.notdolly.com/

Vicki Wiklerson

https://vickiwilkerson.blogspot.com/2022/02/my-year-without-facebook.html?m=1#comment-form

Pete Lawson

www.irishcockroach.com

Rob Garcia

www.shiftlifedesign.com

Stella Parton

https://www.stellaparton.com

Patrik Simpson and Pol Atteu
www.gownandoutinbeverlyhills

REFERENCES/RESEARCH

U.S.A. article
https://www.usatoday.com/story/tech/2023/02/23/facebook-jail-overhaul/11322997002/

Sky News Article
https://news.sky.com/story/facebook-fan-page-rules-deal-devastating-blow-to-tribute-acts-and-impersonators-12851980

Article Facebook Jail Why It Happened and How to Avoid It
www.onehourprofessor.com

Sudi (Rick) Karatas, also the author of Rainbow Relatives and How Catering Sucked The Life Right Out Of Me grew up in Syosset Long Island, now residing in southern California for over two decades. He's also a screenwriter and producer (Walk A Mile In My Pradas) and songwriter and a coordinator for NSAI (Nashville Songwriters Association).